FROM
SEA
TO
HIGH "C"

PAUL JOHANNES VOLKMANN
AND
BEATRICE CAROLINE VOLKMANN

Fulton Books, Inc.
Meadville, PA

Published by Fulton Books 2020

ISBN 978-1-64654-708-1 (paperback)
ISBN 978-1-64654-709-8 (digital)

Printed in the United States of America

CONTENTS

ACKNOWLEDGMENTS

I wish to extend my thanks to my sister, Elizabeth Ann Marshall, who had the original manuscript "And Where Are You from, Little Girl?" transcribed and bound, so copies could be distributed among relatives; and brother, Dr. Robert A. Volkmann, who made sure all my P's and Q's were in order.

INTRODUCTION

What you are about to read is a true story. A few names of certain individuals and places have been changed when their exact names and/or locations were not known. This historical manuscript documented by my mother in book form was handed to me by a relative who asked if I could look it over and "possibly do something with it." I decided to rewrite the book titled *And Where Are You from, Little Girl?* Most of what would be rewritten remains verbatim, for the exception that I would turn the first person "I," for example, into the third person "she," "mom," or "Mother." What I did was to add clarification to parts of her book, translating German words into English, defining classifications of the Nazi regime, and adding fictitious transitory paragraphs that should help readers understand the progressions from one place to another. Not only did I learn a lot about history, but more so a smattering of our mother's life before I was born.

This book is about my mother, Beatrice Caroline Fabricius, who aspired to be a singer. That quest began in the United States in the 1930s and then took her to Germany on the recommendation of a relative in New York. Studying abroad brought a number of surprises. Her initial instructors, a husband-and-wife duo, turned out to be ardent Nazis, who tried to encourage her into becoming a member of the Nationalistic Party. She, however, had no interest in the latter. She had made the journey to Europe to become an accomplished singer.

In the course of her studies, she fell in love with a "man of her dreams" from Holland, only to be faced with a dilemma in their relationship that she never saw coming. Only after untangling the spiderwebs did she eventually set her mind solely on music, again hoping to climb the ladder to accomplishing her goal.

As the daughter of Dr. and Mrs. Julius Fabricius, she was born on June 22, 1914, and spent her childhood in New York City, rural New York, and in Germany. Her father was a family physician, practicing in the Bronx. She had a brother who died in his early childhood. Her parents endured pain throughout their lives from this loss.

Bea, as she was known to many of her friends in later life, enjoyed nature in those early years and developed a passion for music, which led her aspiration to be a singer.

In 1940, she married Ernest W. Volkmann. Thereafter, she would turn her attention to raising three children: me, the eldest; Robert, two years younger; and Elizabeth Ann, informally known as Betsy, five years my junior. The family would end up growing up in Pittsburgh, Pennsylvania, as well as its suburbs. My father was a chemical engineer at Kopper's Company, Verona, Pennsylvania. He later would lead a small company in the chemical and petroleum fields, Fractionation Research, Inc. That led to a move of the family to Bartlesville, Oklahoma, and the parents set up residence there while three of us were hitting the books in college.

The last thirty years of Mom's life were spent in Western Pennsylvania. During the latter part of this period, she was bedridden. Despite her medical issues, she maintained a full and active life; reading, writing, and volunteering her time and energy to many causes.

She was a champion of the poor and disadvantaged, and her life was a devoted to furthering the cause of peace and well-being for all. Her enthusiasm, compassion, and interests had no boundaries. Despite medical problems, she maintained her independence and close relationship with immediate and distant family members.

In addition, she wrote three books: *A Collection of Sing-A-Songs and Selected Writings, The Life of Ernst Wilhelm Volkmann,* and *Where Are You From, Little Girl?* Since only a few copies were printed of each for the family only, it is my belief that the latter book would have widespread interest.

Mom's walk-through history, described in this book, opened my eyes. One will also discover, by reading it, the various challenges my mother overcame after voyaging overseas on various trips and being taught by well-known singing instructors in Loerrach, Germany. Inside the studio, she would be singing the full octave, including such notes from low C to high C. Outside the studio, she was experiencing life during the rise of Adolf Hitler.

Little by little, she sensed an environment that she wanted no part of. Prior to the beginning of World War II, she safely boarded an ocean liner and returned to the United States. There, she could not only look back as to her experiences in that part of Western Germany, but on life in general.

Our mother passed away November 15, 2003.

Born on September 7, 1943, I, passionately, was a photographer of fifty-four years, author, artist, past contributor to law enforcement, and a journalist for fifty-six some years. I have served as a columnist for the *Latrobe Bulletin* (PA) newspaper, featuring *Off the Wall*, where I share my opinions about just about anything and *Inside the Outdoors*, educating readers about members of the animal community that mainly live outside and ways to restore and improve the environment. Both columns have worldwide readership. In addition, I have worked for four other newspapers and national publications.

"Mr. Pee Vee," as I am known by young and old alike, not only in my hometown of Latrobe, Pennsylvania, but also to many throughout the country, graduated from Oakmont High School in 1962, and moved on to Ashland College where I received Bachelor of Arts Degrees in Psychology and Sociology in 1967. I was one of seventeen who was also chosen to receive the Who's Who in Colleges and Universities, an award given in recognition of outstanding campus leadership and the achievements that accompanied it. In 1973, I married my wife, Teri. We were together for forty-three and one-half years until her passing in 2018.

As this book is read, it is with hope that through my efforts, one may realize that this time period involved not only a war between countries, but also a mindset of individual thinking of people in all walks of life. By spelling out my mother's adventures and challenges in this very crucial part of our history, I can only hope that my efforts will prove noteworthy to the point that even the slightest bit of knowledge that may have gone unknown is now revealed, and her efforts in the context and the period of time she lived in are better understood.

Paul Johannes Volkmann II

Caroline and Mother taken from a passport

CHAPTER ONE
LOVED THE WOODS

The year was 1927.

The sun had risen in Loerrach, Germany, one cool June morning. Everything throughout the city sounded peaceful, the air had a slight chill, and as always the birds were making their presence known, for they too were very early risers. Inside the Fabricius home, on the other hand, was a bit of a stir, for Julius and Caroline were preparing to host a small birthday gathering for their daughter, Beatrice, who just turned thirteen.

Hearing the youth exit her room, her mom hurried to the kitchen, clutched the plate holding the cake, and then headed back to the living room where everyone would be singing, "Alles Gute Zum Geburtstag, Alles Gute Zum Geburtstag, Alles Gute Zum Geburtstag zu Beatrice, Alles Gute Zum Geburtstag." The song was followed by applauding and cheering. It was surely a happy time in the family residence where the start of the day was different than the others. Beatrice hastily opened her presents; her smiles were ear to ear. One could feel her sincerity as she thanked each person who gave her a variety of gifts from apparel to jewelry. It wasn't long thereafter that Julius, a physician in the community, had to rush to his family practice located in the same city they lived.

Outside their home, one could definitely sense that nothing of political significance seemed to be taking place during the course of that year, even for those of German descent. Mother was told by her parents that the new cauldron of war had not yet begun to boil, nor had the necessary flame of hatred from Hitler ignited yet. His name actually was not on anyone's lips. She was assured that people in the

Western world were surely blessed with the fact that they valued their peace and thanked God daily that they were given such a blessing. Julius and family had arrived in Deutschland, planning to make the area where he and his family settled his and their place of retirement. He had put in many years as being a doctor. It was time to shelve his little black bag.

Days prior to the birthday party, he had convinced his wife that this would be their last trip across the ocean. Lowering her chin and raising her eyebrows a tad, she stated with a smirk on her face, "Are you sure this will be the last move?"

Julius looked sternly and nodded affirmatively, as he too believed this would be their final resting spot. No sooner did they all settle down on a Thursday did our mother find herself enrolled in a school, that coming Monday.

Attired in a red-flocked dress, which hung well below her knees and fitted with black-and-white saddle shoes, and carrying a small case very much as we today may refer to it as an attaché case, Caroline escorted her daughter approximately one mile to the Loerrach Grundschule (elementary school) along the cobblestone road. As they walked together, they pointed out to each other different plants, animals, and structures that Germans may have taken for granted, but to them, they were "distractions of learning."

When they got to the school building, they ascended six stairs that were constructed by using fifteen- by seventeen-feet-long planks. They were spaced above each other, nine inches apart. Once the pair got to the front, Caroline pulled the handle on the swinging structure, and she and her daughter entered the building. Met immediately by presumably the principal, Hans Beckermann, Caroline introduced her daughter to the long-faced slim gentleman wearing long brown slacks that stopped short of his ankles. Long gray stockings covered his legs and feet, as much as was shown extending out of his shoes.

Since school was already in progress when she entered, it was very difficult for my mother to acclimate her knowledge to that of her fellow students who had been studying various subjects since the beginning of the school year. To be plopped into the whirlwind of activity without so much as a little education preparation, was very difficult for her, to say the least. When Beckermann led her into the classroom, he escorted her behind a large standing map where she was told to sit down, exposing only her footwear. Fellow classmates stated that they had never seen blue and white saddle shoes before. "What do you suppose the rest of her looks like?" seemed to be the number one question. When she was allowed to step out from behind the map and be seen by her new classmates, they could see that Mom was wearing a purple dress. Right away, their minds wandered a bit, and they all concluded that perhaps she had come from the circus.

After exiting from behind the protective shield, she was confronted by a pleasant, apple-faced teacher whom asked, "And where are you from, little girl?" Beatrice's reply was "I come from America," followed by an astonishing reply, "Oh, Mecca, Saudi Arabia!" Since her knowledge of German was limited, she thought to herself right then and there, *I realized I should have devoted more time in practicing my guttural r's, instead of perfecting the more musical "Umlaut" "oe" sound in the word Goethe.*

Even though she couldn't speak the language, she tried her best to fit in by wearing a white dress shirt strangled by a tie, in addition to an abbreviated sport jacket. Since wearing shorts to school was "the thing," Mother wore one of four different pairs that hung in her shallow-depth, oak closet in her house.

When recess mercifully, finally, arrived, three giggling girls towed her from the classroom. They meant no harm, but actually helped her as they shared part of their sandwiches with her. To sustain her mornings, Mom was given small pieces of sausages and cheese from the girls' lunch bags. In addition, she was handed huge slices of bread that were earlier carved from the loaves that could be seen plated on windowsills of German homes. Hesitantly, but thankfully, she accepted the morsels, which she ate almost immediately. As she sat next to her new friends, she could barely make out on a distant street youth, arms coupled, knees high, and faintly hearing the sounds of feet pounding on the stone. Making no sense as to what that was all about, her attention was diverted, and she continued playful activities.

After recess, all youth headed back into the building and made way to their respective classrooms. She was shocked when she saw some students had blocked the entrance to her room. These teens were from other classrooms as well. They had come to gape at her, a young girl from America. From what she learned later would be that this was the first American they had ever seen. Not knowing what to expect, using a bit of persuasiveness, Mother was able to get back into her room. Thoughts went through her mind, however. *Should I go and sit in my assigned seat or sit once again behind the map where I was originally placed by the principal?* All doubts went out of her mind when the no-nonsense apple-faced teacher came to her aid. It became clear immediately that she, for one, had no intention of letting a young newcomer, be she from Mecca or America, disrupt her class. She applied the first determination by showing no leniency toward her faulty German grammar later on. Mom felt that she was one of the few teachers, to whom, in retrospect, she owed a great deal.

Day two brought even more challenges, particularly since she went to school open-minded, figuring that the worst was behind her. No sooner did she get into the schoolyard did a clique of girls guide her off to one side, stating, "You must not associate with those others. Those country bumpkins are not of your class." Mom was a little dumbfounded. She, having been a student in a one-room schoolhouse in New York, never was introduced to the word *class*. It was definitely foreign to her. She began to wonder what status she held, and which classmates were that were in her grouping. There were a group of girls that lived near her house that she made friends with. Joining forces with them, they all walked to school together, having fun, seeing the same sights and sharing their thoughts as they neared the Schulhaus, German for schoolhouse. Some of them included the Stoll Candy Company, and a railroad station, which unleashed a stream of students who had come from outlying villages and towns to attend the two schools of higher learning. One was the Gymnasium, where Latin and Greek were taught, and the other, "Realschule," that emphasized modern languages.

Being the daughter of German parents was sure an advantage in learning the language, Mother mentally concluded. However, she was totally unprepared for a parallel-running language, what it seemed to her only vaguely resembling German. What she learned from her writings was that she was being taught German spoken by the ancient tribe of "Alemannen," of which the native inhabitants were especially proud. "Schwyzerduetsch," the language of the Swiss, was very similar. Part of our mother's homework was learning poems by heart by famous poets. She didn't do well, but on the other hand, her recitation was a never-ending source of good-natured merriment. Her classmates all laughed together at her feeble attempts of repositioning her tongue and forcing her throat muscles to produce unfamiliar sounds.

One day in school, she was asked to get up in front of her class and, no less, hiss the American "th" sound and produce a gentle "r." Efforts proved fruitless, however, which resulted in her having to get a tutor to help her meet her goals. Keep in mind, the class was way ahead of her in conjugating verbs, so every bit of help Mom could get would be a plus in helping achieve the necessary knowledge to move forward enough so that she and the other student would be on the same level.

Not only did she welcome the idea but was very excited about having someone to help her. She quickly realized that her parents were a real asset to her in her youth. This would not be her first one by any means. On the upside of it all, she considered having tutors a real plus. She always considered them as deserving a special place with angels! Finding one within the community of their new home, the person assigned to her was considered an intellectual eccentric, as was her professor husband. Seemingly not quite of this world, Frau (a German woman) Bleistift lived three-quarters of a mile from the Fabricius homestead. When Caroline took her daughter there to be tutored, they were awestruck by the surroundings in which the house stood. There, down somewhat in a valley, stood a cottage covered with vines with neglected, overgrown gardens on either side.

As the two cautiously walked down the stone pathway to the house, they neared the timber-framed, one-story house. Walking around to its side, both quickly came upon the door, and Caroline knocked with her right-handed knuckles. In no time at all, a medium-sized woman with black hair, unblemished features, and deep-seated eyes pulled open the inside door and with a big smile invited the visitors into her house. The three briefly talked, and then Caroline departed. Mom was led over to a small area in the living quarters where two chairs and a small table stood. Each person had her own seat. There, her tutoring began.

A regular schedule was devised, and she visited the Bleistift home as often as time allotted. And it goes without saying, Mother took delight in every visitation. "Frau B.," as she wanted to be addressed, became recognized as a woman with such gentle persuasiveness and tremendous, indefatigable patience that she looked forward to all her lessons. Thanks to this teacher's persistence, the American newcomer received a commendation at an assembly when the school year was over. In the short amount of time during which Mom was tutored, some German stuck, not only temporarily, but she would remember bits and pieces all through her life. That spoke volumes for the aid of Frau B.

She not only looked forward to her weekly tutoring classes, but also spending time in school classrooms was also a plus. She saw it as a never-ending adventure. Mother was very happy living and school-ing in such a friendly environment among the gentle, kind people of southern Germany. Class outings with teachers became highlights of the school year. One of those trips stands out particularly in the mind of this young foreigner. Strangely, it precipitated what could be perhaps considered a mini "Thirty-Year-War." The location was a little chapel that sat atop a small knoll. It was cool and serene inside, and all of the "tired pilgrims" paused there to rest. Suddenly, there was a commotion and giggling near the font of holy water. Asking fellow students, Mom eventually learned that complaints were made by Catholic girls who reported to their teachers the fact that some students actually touched and applied the fluid upon their foreheads. Unable to grasp the significance of what had happened, she tagged along with her friends and they continued on their way. Thinking nothing of it, a song came to her mind, and without giving it so much as a thought, she decided to add a bit of musical accompani-ment to the otherwise quiet surroundings. No sooner did they start along the path of their next destination did Mother break the silence, singing a song lustily, *When the Romans Invaded the North, de rin, chin, chin, chin, chin.* Later, it was reported to the Catholic principal that this song had been deliberately provocative.

She couldn't understand why it was such a big deal. After all, she was part of a home environment where agnosticism was openly acknowledged. Mom couldn't grasp what all the big fuss was about. But as it was, the reprimands by the principal went on for several weeks. Some girls were repeatedly summoned to the office for interrogation, resulting in an atmosphere of ill feeling that persisted for quite a while. On the other hand, her father ridiculed the event, quoting among others, Jonathan Swift: *We have just enough religion to make us hate, but not enough to make us love.* Somehow, she felt feelings of guilt since she had no defined loyalty to either side.

Those weren't the only divisive, uneasy feelings that our mom experienced. When the movie, *Faust*, by Jonathan Wolfgang van Goethe, came to town, her parents gave her permission to see it, but her friend's parents frowned on their daughter's attendance. During that time period, it was not proper to go to the movies even though the feature was a "classic." The gentleman responsible for the motion pictures definitely had credentials as he was a poet, playwright, novelist, and scientist, to name just a few of his achievements. Since her friend's parents were at odds letting their daughter attend, Mother had a feeling of being uncomfortable with her parents' permissiveness.

Weeks after the school year came to an end, she was blessed by being given a new pair of shoes, these being sturdy "Haffele" boots. Mom was so thankful for the switch, for the thick soles made it easier for her to walk on the cobblestones that were used to path sidewalks and constructing the streets. She was also gifted a sleek, black bike that was recognized as a means of transportation, and not by any means a toy. What joy she had as she pedaled over neighborhood streets, pumping and coasting the various hills and straightaways. Sometimes, some of her friends who lived nearby joined her as they wheeled together.

During that time period, there were hardly any cars to be seen. It was a known fact that bicycles and courting went hand in hand. So it would only make sense, she often pondered in her mind, *Wouldn't be glorious if a boy would descend from his bike and ask if he could walk me home?* It didn't take long from fantasy to turn into reality one year later when boys did enter her life. One of her dates took her to a private dancing class where Schwyzerduetsch, a form of the Swiss-German language was dominant. One could tell she was shy, for being together with lads of her age was something new. She felt so uncomfortable that she held a deaf ear to what her instructor was trying to teach her.

Aunt Dora who accompanied Mother on a trip to Germany.

The classes were always held in the homes of leading industrialists. There, Mom was introduced to the affluent society in Germany. It didn't take long for her to lose her shyness. In quick order she became acquainted with male participants. However, no real relationship developed among any of them. During weekends, when school was not in session, she and her parents would visit a distant relative, Great-aunt Dora and Great-uncle Julius's home for dinner. Mom expressed that if her older cousin, Hermann, could be present, especially for the songfest following everyone's siesta, she would be very appreciative. About two hours later, the gang would meet in the living quarters and commence with songs of merriment. Gathering around the baby grand piano, one of the participants chopped out a tune while the rest annihilated, "The Heavens Declare the Glory of God." Her father and uncle sang their own version of the tune, while the ladies could neither get down to the low notes nor reach the high ones. It went without saying that whenever Mom's cousin was there, they all seemed to giggle a bit through each song. That made for a very happy time during this very special get-together.

Mother's Sundays, in general, were different than the other days, even in Loerrach. Friends were never encouraged to visit. It was a family day, very often given over to "Spaziergaenge" (walks) to a café offering scenic views topped off with a treat of something topped with whipped cream. The procession, which moved with solemnity, consisted of her father, his brother-in-law in the lead, followed by her mother and aunt in the middle, with Arlo, her aunt's obese dog, and Mother bringing up the rear. At the café, her aunt, always on the verge of a diet, was tempted by the richest piece of patisserie. Inevitably, she would say, "I really shouldn't." Just as unavoidably, the rest of them could be counted on responding by coaxing her by stating, "Oh, just a little piece?" She never gave in, however.

Often Julius would sit at his "Orchestrelle" (best known type of player-reed organ) on a rainy Sunday morning. The instrument, with its many rolls, had been his joy. He sometimes spent hours pumping away at this nineteenth-century unit. Snatches of classical music were played this way by Mom, too, when she inserted a roll, and pretended she was an organist. She knew the words to the famous ballad, "The Erl King," by the composer Franz Schubert, and liked to sing it because the lyrics were by Goethe. They told the gruesome tale of a father riding horseback through the woods at night, carrying his delirious child to the doctor. The boy envisioned being enticed by the king of the woodland spirits. Mom thought as she sang these stanzas, "How silly it must have sounded, my tiny voice intoning this dramatic ballad to the accompaniment of the organ, all stops pulled out!"

Two years into being residents of Loerrach, Julius and Caroline decided that this would be a good time for their daughter to have violin lessons. As a result, she found herself on a streetcar to Basel, Switzerland, one day a week. Once there, in order to reach the studio of the maestro, Mom first had to venture through many dark alleys and buildings. Once reaching her destination, her path led her to a little building to the end and left of one very narrow alley. Even though it was quite dark, she made her way following directions she had been given, leading to the front door and her soon to be teacher.

In no time at all, after knocking on wood with primarily her middle-finger knuckle, did it suddenly spring open. There stood an older man, clothes disheveled, with a slightly upturned nose. "Come in," stated the gentleman with a somewhat gruff voice. He welcomed his new student with a half-German, half-Swiss dialect, with words that she later would come to understand as meaning "my beautiful young girl." Upon arriving, she quickly learned some ten minutes later that her teacher was very obnoxious, seemingly part of the antiquity of the alleys and buildings. Shortly thereafter, Marx Meinbert showed her where she was to sit. He then proceeded to tell her about the instrument, how to hold it and grip the bow. A bit of excitement stirred within her. Taking it from his hands, she slowly raised it to her chin and lowered it the chin rest. Grasping the bow adorned with real horsehair used to cover the strings, she lowered it slowly down to connect upon one of four tightly strung catgut strands that produced the melodious sounds that she eagerly awaited. What she didn't expect, however, was his physical advances. With chin in the built-in rest, she proceeded to move the bow away from and then back to her. At the same time, Marx decided to make his moves, slowly inching toward her head, eventually kissing her on the check. She definitely did not welcome this. Exclaiming her disapproval, she shouted, "Stop that, please stop. Beende es!" German for "Quit it!" She learned the expression from fellow students.

When her lessons were over, she left hurriedly, rushing through the alleys, sometimes pretending she was escaping from dangerous pursuers, such as a band of ruffians she had read about in Friedrich von Schiller's *William Tell*. The lines *He must pass through this dark valley…there is no other road to Kuestnacht* went through her mind. Sometimes she was so successful in frightening herself that she ran all the way to the safe haven of the large marketplace. It didn't take long for her to realize she had truly wanted to play the violin to have been willing to put up with Marx. Her enjoyment of the scenery and rides to the romantic old city was, unfortunately, offset by her need to constantly ward off the maestro's amorous advances.

Catching wind of all the activities going on around her as she traveled to Basel and back home, Mom learned about the petty smuggling going on. She heard once of a woman who attempted to smuggle butter under her hat. The day was warm, and her contraband melted, letting her secret shine forth on her embarrassed face. Mother even had the audacity to smuggle a deck of playing cards during her travels from one country to the other. Possibly there wouldn't have been any duty, but she couldn't resist the temptation. She sat on the cards in the trolley and felt wicked!

Mother's journey to Loerrach afforded her many cultural opportunities. It was there she heard her first opera, *Der Freischuetz*. Having the record, she often sang along with one of a character's daughter, Agathe. The American native was informed that there were operettas too. Julius's favorite was *Der Vogelhaendler*, and her's was *Das Drei Maedelhaus*. The latter was a romanticized story of Franz Schubert's life, and it overflowed with his wonderful songs.

As Mother grew into her years as a teenager, she realized by many that she had a real passion for classical music. Listening and learning from Schubert played a major role in her young life from then on. That and her violin lessons landed her a spot in the school orchestra where she played second fiddle. One of his most famous compositions, *Marche Miliraire,* was being practiced when she joined the group. The pianist was a boy named Hans Lindenmann. Soon thereafter, she learned that this young man was the fellow who descended from his bicycle to walk her home. The *Marche Militaire* tune became their song, which he whistled under her window. Thus, a romance began, one that had a nineteenth-century quality, or one that could have taken place as far back as the time as that of the Minesingers? They were similar to German poet-musicians of the twelfth and thirteenth centuries. In any case, they had much in common with the romantic troubadours who composed love songs and pined from the distance.

One of the poems Hans gifted to Mother several years later was titled "When I am dead, do not weep for me." He gave it to her before he joined the Kreigsmarine, the German navy. She often wondered, possibly, did he have a premonition of his early death in Hitler's war? Even more prophetic was his short story titled "The Captain." It started out, "On the bridge stood a block of ice; it was the captain." Did he gain the promotion of being a captain? She had only to wonder. She did receive word, that he did indeed meet his death at sea. And even though she really treasured her time with him, Mom felt that at the age of fourteen, she may have been a bit too young to fully grasp and treasure his penmanship of verse, especially love poems. She had her own style and was also gifted through this method of expression. She desired, though, to write about the gurgling brooks, gentle valleys and mysterious dark woods of the Black Forest.

More enduring were her friendships with girls, especially with Wig, whose nickname was a shortened version of her given name, Hedwig. Her family lived in an old villa called Rosenfels, appropriately so named, since one reached it by ascending a hill covered with old rose bushes and vine-covered trees. Occasionally, Mother would be invited there for tea after school. It was accompanied by black bread and marmalade, but to her it was manna from heaven, because of the friendly atmosphere created by her family. There was a father, a lawyer who was elegant, handsome and young; a mother, serene and obviously adored by her family; an older sister as dark-haired and rosy cheeked, as Wig was blond and pale; and occasionally an older son who, as a fraternity student, bore a "Schmiss" (a scar across his cheek), signifying valor in a duel. Because of her fondness toward Mother, she would often call Mom, "Bea", a nickname given that would last all through her life.

Mother pictured with an unidentified member of the German Army.

Wig's father flirted delightfully with his older daughter and held hands with his wife. They were the dream family of her teens. What a fairy-tale life they led. Hitler's war changed all of this. It was very troubling to the Eastern War Zone. Wig's sister would be incarcerated along with her husband in Yugoslavia for many years because he was on the Germany embassy staff. It would fall on Wig's shoulders to take care of their children. The brother would be counted as missing in Germany.

Living in Loerrach, Mom had no premonition of what lay ahead for Germany. Of communists, widespread poverty, of the unemployed, and the street corner hoodlums, nothing was obviously seen or, as far as that went, felt. In 1929, she sensed a rising tide of nationalism. At one incident, at the assembly marking the end of the school year, Mother, and the others with her, sang the rousing *Wachtaug* chorus from *Die Meistersinger*. What Mom sang, she thought was Richard Wagner's text. Instead, someone had substituted the wording, *the Reich must be allowed to stand just as our forefathers carved it out with swords*. Quite possibly, the groundwork was being laid for the rise of National Socialism, it was surmised.

For some time, Mother's father had been contemplating whether or not for the family to return to America. Instead of heading to the United States as planned, however, she and her parents headed to Heidelberg, Germany, where Julius wanted to hear some lectures at the university there. Thus, her family embarked on another path. Not only would her parents be changing course to that new city, but Mom would find herself packing and heading to a boarding school to where she would continue her education.

Compared with the other boarding schools or homes she visited, the setting of Lernenort Internat was, this time, located in a castle. Mom described it as a large villa, which stretched over a lovely park with many fine old trees. Here, too, could be found an old Gothic chapel. Only the room in its tower was in use. There, the very popular gardening teacher, Walli Wurm, had her inner sanctum. Mother was told by fellow students that it was moldy and dark in the chapel. The student body was not encouraged to visit it.

She actually looked forward to this boarding school. There seemed to be some discord with her parents, and thus, she could escape the tensions at home. Only after arriving there did she have second thoughts, particularly when she imagined it would be fun taking part at dances with fraternity students. It didn't take long to figure out that dances were definitely not on her curriculum.

The year was 1930. It was a day of celebration, especially since this date marked Mother's sixteenth birthday. Instead of being with friends and raising a glass, she found herself sitting in the park, miserably alone, eating a piece of birthday cake sent to her by her aunt. So much different than her former school, there were no giggles to welcome her. In fact, no one seemed to take notice of her presence. Looking around, she saw small groups of girls everywhere chatting or reading under trees. Their voices weren't the pleasant melodious kind to which she had become accustomed to in Loerrach. It didn't take long for her to realize that she had entered an enclave of Prussians. "Why this school?" she often asked herself. After all, we Fabriciuses were neither Prussian nor aristocrats.

Not knowing what to expect from minute to minute became a bit nerve-racking. First, Mother was greeted by Hilda Ohrwurn whose clipped diction coupled with an unpleasant nasality in her voice provided her with a chilling fear that she was being committed to a reform school because of her friction at home with her father. The headmistress must have sensed the uneasiness of Mom, for suddenly her expression changed to a slight smile. "Na, kindchen [little one], we must have you measured for uniforms," she stated. Mother's heart sunk when she heard the uttering of those words. On the other hand, she was encouraged by the fact that the attractive dresses had no resemblance to prison garbs.

In addition to her having new attire, Mother was told that she would be having the engravings of BF10 on her silverware among the crowns and crests and illustrious names on heavy cutlery. Her classmates were primarily from aristocratic North German estates, many of whom had been tutored at home and had come to prepare themselves for their final exams, which, when passed, would give them the "Mittlere Reife" degree. This lacked one year of being equivalent of the American high school diploma. The majority of students were of Mom's age group.

She would be assigned to a dormitory shared by four other girls, one of whom was in her class. She immediately had a rapport with a French girl, Adele, who like her, was a foreigner. Unfortunately, Adele's socialite mother took her to Kiel shortly after our mother arrived. As far as the personalities of her other roommates, she generalized them as being pleasant, and found that actually she was happier there than at any former places. Part of it attributed to the fact that her roommates were a mischievous, fun-loving bunch who, among other escapades, put catnip under the window of the math teacher whose room was in a cottage in the park (with gratifying results!). The warm June nights invited them to frolic and dance after "lights out" in the moonlight. Deciding to make a switch to be with classmates her age, Mother soon learned that the choice would turn out to be a mistake and that she should have stayed where she was assigned.

It was during this period that she and others were all bused to the city of Mainz for festivities celebrating the departure of the French occupation troops, dating back to from the First World War. Huge crowds gathered to listen to the venerable old President von Hindenburg speaking from the balcony. We all sang *Deutschland, Deutschland Ueber Alles.* Emotions ran high. A line Mom remembered especially was *Uns zur edler Tat begeistern* (to inspire us to noble deeds). Following was the chanting of *The Rhine is Free,* of course, in German. Mother expressed to one of the girls that accompanied her, "I never felt so '*Deutsch!*'"

In the fall, another field trip to a political event took place. There she and her fellow students marched into the town hall at Heidelberg, where a man named Adolf Hitler was expected to address a meeting of the National Socialist Party. When they entered, there were no longer any seats, so they stood in the smoke-filled, oven-heated room. Not long after entering, Mom found herself on the huge outdoor balcony of the hall. The only conclusion that occurred to her was that she must have fainted inside. She later learned that a man from the Red Cross dragged her outside so she could get some fresh air. Coming to her senses, she heard a tumultuous applause come from the hall accompanied by the cries of "Sieg Heil!" (say hail). Even though Mom had a tremendous view of the Neckar River below, and its surroundings, she tore herself away to rejoin her group. When she got back with her fellow students, she learned that Hitler had not come as expected, and that everyone in attendance had to listen to a so-called political leader.

Back at boarding school, Mother had a problem with one of her fellow students. Not knowing whom to talk to about this, she mustered up enough courage to go before Ohrwurn and burden her with the complaint. When Mom asked her to release her of her obligation of remaining in school the rest of the year she, to her amazement, was gentle and kind to her, intimating that to persevere in school would be a victory of which she later would be proud. Mother never learned how to cope with a miserable roommate. She did stay and passed her examination and even participated in a trip to Italy. For years, however, she pondered over the kindness given to her by the headmistress, as she came to the conclusion that Ohrwurn had not felt the obligation of molding her into a young Prussian since Mother was an American.

Basel may have introduced Mom to the joys of music, but Florence opened her eyes to visual arts. Under the pictures and the sculptures, she recognized the names of Rubens, Raphael, and Michelangelo, and many others of whom Ohrwurn had spoken. Mom gave her heart to the painter Bartolome Esteban Murillo. His gentle Madonnas and dark-skinned little boys with blue eyes satisfied her romantic nature at that time. She couldn't resist the temptation, whereby she went ahead and purchased one of his smaller renderings.

Looking back before she left that Italian city, every event she recounted left her heart filled with joy. The day before they left Florence, she and her fellow students discovered the street vendors who appreciated their limited Italian and descended upon them like a flock of pigeons, shouting, "Quanta costa? Troppo caro!" (How much? Too much?) Mother came home with a silver bracelet and a charming little Venetian frame for her Murillo Madonna. The memory of this trip to Italy survived as an enchanting experience, independent of her generally, unhappy, bored school days.

The same person to whom Mom sought counsel also conducted worship services at the school. She did so with almost business-like efficiency. Mother learned that most of the girls, no doubt, started their days at home in this fashion, with family and servants all being present. It was definitely a new experience for her. Protestant aristocracy at that time was firmly bonded to the Lutheran Church since the time of the Reformation. It was not surprising that from this segment of the German population, resistance fighters arose. After all, Hitler ranted not only against Jews and Catholics, but at Christianity itself, calling it a foreign religion foisted on the Germans—one that he was determined to eradicate. Mother would later learn that when Ohrwurn read Jewish Psalms for the soldiers on the front during times allotted for worship, she was being spied upon by a baroness's daughter who became registered at the school. This became a revelation. Of consequence, she was forced to resign her position at the school, no less, and later became employed by the Red Cross with the same dedication she had shown toward building up her previous work.

If Mother would have stayed on at that school a second year, she would have come to realize that Ohrwurn had given the institution its name since she was indeed its founder. This was in itself an amazing revelation, for Mom believed the school dated back to the time of the monarchy. Actually, it had only been in existence for only three years when she arrived. It was further learned that the headmistress had no intention of perpetuating the Victorian values of German aristocracy. Quite the contrary. She actually had strong views of providing a broad education for the modern young women, one that would allow them to take their place as equals next to their intellectual husbandss. In her earlier life, she had met many women who were pioneers in forging a new social order in Germany, even before World War I and, especially, however, during the early years of the Weimar Republic.

It seems Ohrwurn's father's seminars rubbed off a tad on his daughter. He had leading sociologists, theologians, and political scientists for study groupings at his estate. One pastor, turned sociologist, Friedrich Siegmund-Schulze was especially an interesting man.

He had relinquished his prestigious position as pastor of the elite church in Potsdam in order to devote himself completely in pursuing his dedication to new social programs. Having had many ideas on how to alleviate the plight of the working class, he therefore gave lectures all over Germany on this subject.

Germany was changing, Mother recounted that at one occasion, Hitler, before he had seized power, appeared with an entourage of his "SA." hitmen (assault division). Apprehension seized the audience, but to everyone's surprise, there was no disturbance, for Hitler could be heard muttering, "I like what this man is saying." He actually appropriated Schulze's word, *Volkgemeinschaft*, which interpreted meant, "community of the people." Unlike Hitler, however, Schulze's aim was not to promote a more egalitarian society but to transform it later into an efficient war machine. After Hitler became "Reichskanzler" (chancellor), he offered Schulze the position of "Minister of Culture," but the former pastor who was only too aware by then of Hitler's ideology turned down this appointment resulting in his having to flee for his life. He moved to Switzerland. It was there that his daughter and family often visited him. Actually, it was this connection, that in a convoluted way, led to Ohrwurn's arrest and ultimate execution.

Mother's boarding school

In 1931, after Mother graduated from boarding school, Julius finally decided to take his family back to America. During their last weeks in Heidelberg, they were treated to a spectacular celebration, staged by the fraternities of the university. There were torchlight parades, much singing, and colorful floats on the Neckar River. Thinking back, there was much that stood out in Mom's mind as she gave thought to her past. One particular deeply moving experience seemed to surface, one that would have a far-reaching effect on her later life. Ever since she and her parents had gone to Germany in

1927, she had formed a deep attachment to her uncle. He had a son, Sebastian, her age. They loved to climb trees and romp through the woods together. Like most children of the family, life with them was a very exciting adventure. Her so-called Uncle Alwin was the head forester of the region and the family, as well as the forestry, were housed in an old castle in the midst of the charming Palatinate countryside. Besides Sebastian, there was a much older daughter, Ingrid, and two older sons, Manfred and Peter. It was, however, the rustic uncle with his hearty laugh and boisterous way she adored. His wife, Erica, was always ready to join in the merriment. Their carefree air made the life of a teenager a splendid adventure. To their misfortune, they had lost a child, a girl, that Mom thought must have resembled her because they called her their "chosen" daughter. It was in fellowshipping with the family that she learned of Ohrwurn's untimely death. Through them they had learned that this individual who was so kind to Mother led another life. She had been a dedicated Nazi in the 1930s even before Hitler rose to power.

Questions entered Mother's mind as time went on in Germany. Was anti-Semitism not endemic to German aristocracy? Why did Ohrwurn have to suffer with such an extreme punishment? Only after researching the matter some years later did Mother learn that the former headmistress was very compassionate to not only the Jewish people, but all suffering humanity. What Hitler ended up doing to her was deplorable beyond anyone's imagination. She was kept in a frigid cell, always in handcuffs, and interrogated night and day for weeks on end. Treated like a common criminal, she was given very little food. An effort was made to connect her with the group that had tried to assassinate Hitler, and none was found. Until the end, her family believed she would be exonerated since the evidence against her was indeed so meager. The verdict was eventually reached. She was convicted of being an enemy of the state, and her death was eminent. When her kin learned that she met her demise by being beheaded, her friends and relatives found it to be incredulous. Ohrwurn, herself, had only concern for others during her last weeks. Right up to the last minute, she was heard reciting Psalms. The pastor was with her and saw her go with quiet fortitude to her death. For a long time, Mother found it difficult to reconcile her death.

It was late April when Mom made another visit to Alvin and Erica's. Staying overnight, she slept in a huge bedroom in which it was said that Johan Christoph Friedrich von Schiller had written a famous poem, *Auf Dem Wege zum Elsenhammer*. Mother was overwhelmed by his thought and was much too excited to even consider doing any sleeping. Often, she would rise before the others were awake, and rush into the burgeoning forests at dawn. Once when she arrived at her favorite spot, deep in the woods, she sank into the moss and experienced a surge of happiness such as she had never felt since. The forest was a temple in which she felt very close to her Creator. Someone had intimated that her grandfather, who was also a forester, might have had a hand in planting the now seen tall trees. She knew him only from his picture but nonetheless felt very close to him. In the evening, her uncle would take her to the rustic watchtowers in the trees from where everyone could observe the wild animals as they came forth to drink. Mother remembers, vowing at that time, that she would return to this spot where she hoped to spend the rest of her life. Then looking down, shrugging her shoulder a tad and changing from a grin to a frown, she faced the reality and knew it was never to be. After all, in a few weeks, she realized, she and her parents would be sailing to the United States.

Farewell, dear friends, dear forest…

Julius and Caroline on a swing at their White Plains, New York, farm.

Chapter Two
Medical Practice Again?

It took Hitler and the Second World War to remove the burden of decision-making for all of them. Friends often said how exciting and broadening Mom's gypsy-like life must have been. Few appreciated the many heartaches of goodbyes or the unpleasant experience of being confronted so often with new, unfamiliar lifestyles in both countries. She compared herself to a young plant that really couldn't endure too much transplanting. As Mother saw it, "When I was in Germany, I was an American, and when I was in the USA, I was a German!"

As they set off on an ocean liner, Mom recalled the choppiness of the waves and the views of endless waters. At times the waters were calm, and on other occasions, they were quite turbulent. It was almost as though the waters were imitating the emotions from which they left behind. Mom had found a certain placidity in the Black Forest. As the Hitler Regime was building, its ugliness was leaving waves of turmoil that were mounting on the streets.

Mother became immediately aware of the various circumstances upon docking. In New York, no one welcomed her at the pier. The cacophony of city noises was brutal in its assault, and she felt little kindness toward her father for bringing them back to America.

After being transplanted from a country, being taken over by the makings of the Nazi Party, and feeling the uneasiness of the people in various surroundings, Mother sensed that being back in her own stomping grounds in the United States was anticlimactic. Much had happened during her teenage years in Germany. The gigglers who helped her initially cope with a new beginning in her first schooling experience, her trips to and from the lewd maestro in Basel where she got her start learning how to play the violin, and her main stay at the boarding school, all must have played in her mind over and over again as she and her parents set up residency in the United States.

Inasmuch as Mother grew up in this country, she couldn't help but share some of the past memories with her mother. The name, Mum, seemed to be handed down through an inheritance if one would call it that. So in speaking to her mother, she stated, "Mum, do you remember us moving to a farm near Somoken, New York, when I was five?"

"Yes, dear," she replied.

Pondering a bit more, Mom stated, "And do you remember when I was asked to be a flower girl at Aunt Maria's wedding?"

Mum smiled and nodded her head up and down. All her thoughts seemed together at once. "Do you remember the singer who was asked to perform?" Again, an affirmative nod resulted. She was asked to sing a specific German song of which it turned out that it was one of a few she knew. It became our understanding that it mattered not as to what stanzas she chose, for, according to her bit of "wisdom," any stanza sung would sound just as good as those requested as "the real thing." But what Aunt Maria didn't know was that Mother, Julius, and Caroline could not only speak German fluently but understand it as well. So when translated into English, Aunt Maria learned that the title of her song was "My Love Has Left Me." Part of one of the stanzas noted, *the ring she gave me has fallen apart.* Needless to say, she was not very pleased with this song choice. As a matter of fact, she resented it until the day she died.

Right after the wedding, the family pulled up stakes and moved to a farm near Kingston, New York, some distance away from their original homestead, this time in the Catskill Mountains. Their new home consisted of a house in the valley that was given the name "the winter house" and a white-boxed structure of a building on top of a nearby hill called "the summer residence." Even though it was called a farm, the family never did any farming. Mom remembers both houses to be very primitive with no running water, electricity, telephones, and indoor plumbing. The summer house even had its stairs to the second floor on the outside. It led to a balcony. On rainy days, one needed an umbrella to go to bed.

Julius and his chauffeur made the trip first. They carted along Mom's goat and her bantam chickens that were gifts from his patients in the Bronx. It was recommended that he relocate in the country after he suffered a breakdown as a result of overwork. Later his wife and Mother followed to set up housekeeping.

When Mother was six, she attended a one-room schoolhouse approximately two miles from the farm. After school or on weekends, she would roam one hundred acres close to and a bit farther away from home. She would return, on occasion, toting newts and small snakes, much to her mother's dismay. Her father spent days picking berries in the woods or hammering away at stone walls in search of fossils, which were found to be abundant.

And even though Julius had an easy go of it, Mom's goat gave her a real challenge. Sometimes it broke loose from the long rope, finding its way over to the strawberry patch, eating every last one of these tasty fruits. It even climbed the rafters in the barn, once ascending up to an area where hay was once stored only to fall through the slats, landing on the canvas roof of the family car parked in the barn, going through the material and landing on the back seat. Her "precious" pet even broke Mother's little finger when it became interlocked in its horns. It was very much a blessing for Mom to have a father who was a doctor. Julius immediately took care of her wounds. He then anaesthetized the animal and sawed off its horns. Soon thereafter, when Mom went back to school, she couldn't wait to show off her splint that had been affixed to her finger.

Her teacher, Ruby Cure, was not much older than the oldest boys in the class. It became rather obvious in the springtime that she had absolutely no control over these youth as they kept jumping out of the windows. Her lack of being a disciplinarian caused her to be replaced by a new teacher, Mrs. Lana van Tassle. She had recently been widowed and liked to play on the harmonica and have her students sing such sad songs with such stanzas as *Kind words will never die, never die, though in the grave*. Mom and she became very close to the point of becoming the teacher's pet.

Neither ice, snow, nor peril of night could have kept Mom away from school. She loved it! One advantage of attending a one-room schoolhouse was listening to what the older students were learning. One subject, long-division, captured her attention the most. She became fascinated with the numerical patterns.

It's always been common knowledge that when the season of Christmas was in the air, there was much excitement from young and old alike. Paper cutouts, the erection of trees, and the adorning of decorations in and outside the school building as well as the stores and homes in Kingston were everywhere. One of Mother's favorite memories was helping decorate the town's community house with pine boughs. Others hung mistletoe at various locations. And it goes without saying, there were always girls chased about as the fellows stood around those hanging plants.

In the spring, when the sap rose, family and friends got together to tap the maple trees. Mom's job was to stand by if needed to help carve the little reed pipes that would be inserted into the trees, allowing the secretion to channel out. After it all was collected, the sap was brought back to the house where Caroline would boil the tiny watery plant juice all day long on a woodburning stove, resulting, disappointingly, in a half a pint of thick syrup. There never was any question about it. She was a hard worker, all right, and put her heart and soul into working on this farm.

In the early twenties, Caroline got very sick. Julius decided to take her back to Europe to find a cure for her ailment. The family of three packed their bags and headed once again to the seaport to catch an ocean liner across the great Atlantic Ocean. Their destination would be, once again, Germany.

Picked up by Mom's uncle, Joachim Ludwig, a judge, they accepted the invitation to stay at his house in Metropole. He had an apartment above his courtroom. After they toted their bags up the staircase, unpacked, and carefully put away their belongings, Mom began to peer out the window with great curiosity. Commenting to her parents, she stated, "I can see across the courtyard and actually look into the prison cells."

It became apparent that Mom was still a minor, and she would need some additional schooling while they were in this foreign country again. Inasmuch as there was no determination as to how long it would take for Julius to find the cure for his wife, it became apparent that tutoring was in order for their daughter. Finding the best in the neighborhood, the nine-year-old student had to walk daily, feeling fraught with danger, to the house of Fraeulein Valerie Vater. She either passed a chained, snarling dog or a French soldier, who was there as a part of the army of occupation after the First World War, or watch a countryman attempt to eat crispy Schnitzels usually walking in the opposite direction. What created the fear within Mom when she saw that soldier wearing a dark-pea-green uniform, standing erect and holding a rifle, to the day she died, could offer no explanation. In any case, she was always relieved when she reached the dwelling place of her teacher. Mom pretty much stayed to herself to and from her home.

Just as the merriment existed in Kingston, such was the same when the month of December made its debut in Metropole. As usual, Mom saw the Christmas season as a delightful time for a little girl. Her Aunt Dora used to make tiny cakes for her dolls. On Christmas Eve, when the sound of a small bell rang, it would signify that the Christ Child had been there and left presents. But not only did Christ's birth signify a very significant event of the year, but also Julius had finally found the appropriate drug, dosing Caroline with it at regular intervals until she regained her health. Once again, the family decided to return to America where they could resume their activity on the farm.

Unsettled about his retirement, Julius felt inclined to return to his medical practice. Since he felt strong enough and had the willingness to start anew, farm life became a thing of the past, and a new residency was sought, this time in White Plains, New York, where he would find himself as busy as he was in the Bronx. Mom saw this span as the most normal period of her childhood. She actually liked her new living arrangement. "We finally returned to civilization," Mother stated. School was just around the corner, she gained many friends in no time at all, and her mother could have her afternoon teas again. Mom even joined a church by herself. Her parents chose to do other things on Sunday mornings. Julius used to reserve that time of the week to service his vehicle. Of consequence, often he could be seen fiddling with something while lying on his back on the driveway under the car. That was a time set aside to grease up the instruments.

Apart from the family's unorthodox observance of the Sabbath, they conformed more or less to the mores of, what was then, small-town America. More so, my mom was convinced she would spend the rest of her life in White Plains. In so doing, she asked her parents whether she could have a dog for a pet. Having a dog for not only her to love, but also for the rest of the family to do the same, would be a welcome edition. However, when Mom popped the big question to her mother, she did not expect to get the answer she received. "No, you had better not have a dog. You may have to leave it behind if we move again. Her thoughts were thwarted when she realized White Plains was only a temporary spot, and it may be sooner than later that moving on would be in the cards.

Caroline, Julius, and family

Chapter Three
"Dear Platty"

Julius found a nice apartment facing Broadway on the ninth floor of the building. The back of it faced the Hudson River. Often, he would take guests down a hallway to a large picture window, whereby sightseers could see a major part of the city with the river running through it. As he pointed out the locations of various buildings, one could easily sense that his heart was truly into it. Mom wasn't so fortunate. Her bedroom was in the back with nothing to be seen outside the transparent, plain-glass glazing. On the other hand, she felt blessed to have a roof over her head, the conveniences of home living, not to mention no threats of fearing for the family's or her life. On the other hand, sleeping was a little hard getting used to. It seemed that right outside the windows were howling cats, irate shrieks of tenants who poured pails of water on these creatures and screaming, belching out to other people somewhere in their midst. It did prove one thing. The building was surely inhabited by other human beings.

At first it took a little doing for Mother's family to get acquainted to other tenants. The elevator operators were very friendly to her. One of them especially impressed her because he could whistle "double stops" as he moved the mechanical device either up or down the shaft. As a physician, knowing medicine was not new to my grandfather. However, being in a new city meant reestablishing himself so people would not only know that he was highly educated, but also that he had the expertise to come to the aid of those who needed his services. It certainly didn't take long for word to get around. Before long, Julius could be seen passing out medicines and giving free advice each day after coming home from his office. Those were the days before Social Security and Medicare, and there was very little free medical help for the poor.

Having a bit of imagination, Julius applied his handiwork to fix up one of the rooms where the family lived. Mom occasionally peeked in and, to her astonishment, was amazed and awestruck in seeing the standing-room only crowd that filled the room, each patiently waiting to be seen. At the end of the day, he would leave one room and strode toward the dining room where Caroline had fixed a wonderful meal for him before he headed out to make house calls. "Be very quiet," her daughter was warned, "so your father will not be disturbed while eating."

One day while she and her mother were having tea together in the dining room, Mom asked her where she was born. "In the Bronx," she said, "in a part called University Heights."

Then, with a chuckle Caroline stated, "My father diagnosed you as a tumor, since she was already in her forties. But as you see, it certainly turned out differently." The two statements resulted in a hearty laugh from both women!

Uneducated as to the pros and cons of medicine, Mother admitted that she didn't have a clue. She was quick to admit, "I was still quite young during this period. I never took an interest in medicine. After all, I was a visitor in my own country."

Coming off two intoxicating experiences, one to Florence, Italy, and another to a German forest, it seemed in the back of Mom's mind she wondered, *Is this another temporary stop, or would I be taking my belongings somewhere else in the not-too-distant future?* Mom still possessed souvenirs from overseas, one a photograph of a statue of David by Donatello taken in Italy, and miscellaneous memorabilia from Germany.

One of the distractions that burdened both the doctor and his wife, on a day-to-day basis, were the everyday occurrences in Germany. National Socialism was sweeping the country with Hitler at its helm. Mom's mother was very concerned about her relatives there. She spent many tearful hours packaging huge containers with food to ship overseas, so our many relatives there would not starve to death. When she wasn't reaching out to relatives, part of Caroline's outreach included inviting the daughter of their black chauffeur to go with Mom to the circus when it came to town. She viewed this event as a far happier one than attending a concert given by a famous neighbor, Werrenrath, who was a fine baritone. A little giggle followed after she recalled this memory.

One recollection led to another until this story surfaced. "One of my great joys in those days," Mother said, "was to visit my Uncle Will at the Museum of Natural History where he was a curator of mammals. There he would invite Mother to go behind the scenes to see the fossilized eggs of dinosaurs. She looked down at them in awe, for they were so much larger than the ones she was used to seeing when her mother took her shopping at the market!"

He was known to fellow employees and the general public as William K. Gregory. His family came from England and settled not far from where the institution was located and was the leading authority on evolution—and mammalian identification—at that time. In the course of his research, he would come to write a book on his findings, titled *From Fish to Man*.

When fall arrived, once again, Mom would find herself enrolling in a school curriculum again. This was her senior year. She would be attending a private school known as St. Agatha School, in Brooklyn, New York. Mother's language focus was French, no less. She knew a little bit of the language and spoke with a certain French dialect. One of her science classes included physics. Mother was quick to admit that she lacked the necessary background education to move forward with this class. Leave it to her, she pursued the task and found herself a tutor who was of great help.

Life seemed to be traveling along on an even keel, when suddenly tragedy struck. Mom was not allowed to continue her classes. Her father, considering her ill, took her out of school. Rhonda Erskine, her teacher, did not feel that Mother should drop out just because there existed this health "suspicion." Erskine pleaded with Caroline to allow her daughter to remain in school and pursue more subjects along the line of writing, as she saw certain qualities that prompted her to state, "Be sure that you send your daughter to college to become a writer." She then added, "If I had a daughter who liked to write as much as yours, I wouldn't care if she ever brushed her teeth!"

During her brief attendance at St. Agatha, however, Mother made two lifelong friends, who ended up as notable musicians in New York.

Julius consulted various specialists in connection with my mother's illness, but no diagnosis of significance could be made. In retrospect, Mom suspected that modern medicine would have discovered she had chronic fatigue syndrome and perhaps some "culture shock." She should have gone back to school. However, by then, her parents had enrolled her in the Platt School of Music where she took violin and singing lessons. Also located in Brooklyn, she received a taste of the two subjects, but as her education took another turn, she was on the move once again with new challenges.

Because of the amount of stress that was being created during the practice of her father's medical career, he decided to invite another doctor from the city to help him treat the large number of patients who were now filling his waiting room. Dr. Georgios Sniflelodg was asked if he would join Julius during his daily practice. He accepted.

Little did Mother know that this newcomer was a close friend of a woman on the staff at the Platt School of Music. Known affectionately as "Dear Platty," she would become another lighthouse keeper in Mom's life's journey. The analogy of a lighthouse was even more fortuitous, since this institute was housed in the tower of Carnegie Hall building. Class was in a large spacious room, which was subdivided into two studios by folding doors. Instructors received students in the one that had a huge desk on which there were many piles of papers. There too were the remnants of her hastily consumed lunch of cheese and crackers. Mother soon learned she gave little thought to the incidental matter of food. There were so much more matters to address.

First on the list of things to accomplish was an interview with Dear Platty. Caroline accompanied her daughter as the three of them sat down to have a little talk. This time Mom felt she was not confronted by a "statue of granite," referring to her first impression of Fraeulein von Thadden. That memory was embedded in her brain.

45

On the contrary, in this case, her first glance told her Dear Platty was more like a storybook character out of a Victorian novel. Under the mound of gray hair, precariously piled high on her head, were two very lively eyes, a small slightly upturned nose, and lips that were later to observe as incapable of being coerced into a frown. When she spoke, she had the most agreeable of voices. Immediately Mom sensed she was in the presence of someone who was at ease with the Vanderbilts or Rockefellers. But no one with such a delightfully upturned nose could appear haughty or intimidating. Her words gave further assurance of her innate kindness as well as an almost self-deprecating good humor. Her comfortable, ample lacy dress fell in gentle cascades from her shoulders, giving the impression that the many diverse pieces of light fabric had casually arranged themselves as a dress rather than having been coerced by a pattern.

In timely fashion, from around a corner, Mother's music teacher appeared and came over to them both and sat down across from them. Immediately she greeted by stating, "Good morning, Mrs. Fabricius, and to you, Beatrice," emitting smiles to both as she talked. "So you are looking forward to receive lessons involving musical arrangements, are you?" she said, looking at Mom squarely in the eyes. Caroline commenced to talk about her daughter with a tale of woe concerning her pitiful child. As she continued her litany, Miss Platt turned ever so slightly and deliberately winced at Mom.

"I don't believe a word of this," she signaled. And then came an unexpected question. She then said, "Would you like to sing for me?"

Mom's mother was certainly taken aback by this statement, blurting out, "My daughter has come for violin lessons!" Mom thought the whole matter through for a few moments and then stated that she really didn't have a great singing voice.

Miss Platt raised her tone of voice and replied, "Nonsense, everyone has a voice. Come to the piano and sing a scale." Mom did as instructed. After her appraisal, Miss Platt was captivated by what she heard. "You have a very nice little voice," she said. "Why don't you give your daughter a say in this matter, also?" she proposed to Caroline. To Mother's surprise, she consented. At the time, of course, she did not realize that Miss Platt had, perhaps, sensed she was adrift in water over her head. Dear Platty may have picked up on that fact. That gave her even more determination to instill some self-confidence in her new pupil.

As they both learned in short order, Miss Platt would turn out to be only a voice teacher. Charlotte Hall, her colleague, would be her violin instructor. She too was a liberated Victorian lady, but her hair was drawn sternly back into a bun. Over her eyes she wore rimless spectacles. Her feet were attired with high-button shoes with which she resolutely tapped the floor to mark time. In spite of this stern exterior, she was a warm and charming middle-aged woman who also became a friend to Mother. The series of events provided nothing but positive comments from Julius and Caroline at dinner that night. He was intrigued as to how the interview went and how both his wife and daughter thought about each of the teachers. Nothing but good comments were heard from both of them. The ordeal turned into quite a conversation of the day's events.

When Mother entered school for voice lessons, she took one long look at Miss Platt and concluded that she probably was seventy-five years old. She had no way of knowing how successful she was in her younger years as a vocal teacher. Although she certainly had pupils who were far more gifted, Mom gained the impression that she was far more interested in developing character than voices at that stage in her life. Mother would return home every day with stories of instances that transpired at the school. One example was the encouraging pep talks the whole student body got. In a way as she saw it, that in itself was a self-confidence booster, in a matter of speaking. Hall's goal was aimed at positive thinking, a way to instill in her students that they must "go right to the top too," particularly after fellow students had achieved their goals. Mom knew she certainly was very much in need of the remedy her teacher could offer!

It became apparent that as well-meaning as her aims were in providing Mother with self-confidence through singing lessons, Miss Platt's efforts undermined Mother's practicing of the violin for which she had a degree of proficiency. Soon thereafter, however, Mom diligently began singing lessons to the point that she was told to sing at a recital with printed programs, assisted by singers who were quite good musicians. Thus, Mother discovered such famous composers as Schubert, Schumann, Brahms, Franz, Mendelssohn, and many more, all whose songs she sang in her most limited voice. Included were the old Italian favorites and the French "Bergerettes." Her knowledge of German and French made these art songs instantaneous rapture for her. The poetry, the melodies, all spoke of the beloved world. Miss Platt had succeeded in making her believe she could sing. Truly, she felt as though she was an emperor without clothes! She underestimated the enjoyment she would consequently receive in interpreting the lyrics as she voiced her compositions at the various recitals. One thing was for certain. Thanks to Miss Platt, Julius and Caroline's little girl was not only taught arias to sing, but how to become a very talented performer as well.

Mom was heard to have cheerfully stated, "Just as our ninth-floor apartment lifted me above the commercialism of Broadway, so the tower room in Carnegie Hall carried me away on a magic carpet ride into the land of make-believe. Instead of putting down roots in my native land, I pretended I was back in Germany. Thus, I lived two illusions: that I was not only in that country but also, I had a voice!"

Before Mother knew it, she was singing duets with some of Miss Platt's best students. One classmate, in particular, was a baritone who sang perfect German. She was very instrumental in encouraging the duo to sing duets. After a while, Mom began to sense that the German arias were sung just for her. What may have been a debatable subject soon turned into something that she never expected. This gentleman wasn't just someone to share lyrics with her on stage, but someone who would escort her to concerts, operas, and even to record sessions in his home. As a resident of Greenwich Village, Max Cornelius's apartment was not just nine floors above the ground, but to her, much closer to heaven, she would share stories about him with others, many times with a twinkle in her eyes. She also went on bicycle tours with a group of his friends on weekends, usually on Sundays. Part of the destinations included cycling down the deserted Wall Street, past the fish market and then taking the ferry across a nearby river to the country where they would enjoy the wide-open spaces. Mom felt as though she was back in Germany, as this was customary for people of that country, getting about from one place to another. Little by little, her circle of acquaintances increased. She now had two very close friends from the Agatha days. In addition, one like her, Rosemarie, a recently arrived German, who was adopted by an uncle and the other, a piano student whose parents were Greek. She would attend concerts with them as well.

Both enrolled at Columbia University. Both she and her new German friend, Max, signed up for and together took English extension courses. Sometimes, they visited Yorksville, the German section of Manhattan where they listened to a brass band all the while indulging in a bit of nostalgia. Listening to German records while eating way too many Marzipan Pig candies were two of their favorite pastimes.

Although some of her friends' families were well-to-do, Mother never envied their wealth. "My world of fantasy is all I need," one would hear her say upon occasion.

After sailing to Germany and returning to the United States, living here and there, from one place to another, farm to farm, to finally settling down at the most recent place nine floors up, facing Broadway in New York, New York, from one direction to overlooking the Hudson River, very gradually Mom began to feel at home in this large tourist attraction. Excited to show relatives the place where she could finally call home, supposedly, she contacted relatives from various states to join her for a bit of sightseeing in and around the city. The first person she got in touch with was her cousin, Ellen M. Baker, who lived in New Jersey. In a matter of days, she appeared at the family residence. Mother was so excited, she exclaimed, "Let's go while the weather is great!" And so, the two quickly made way to the elevators, lowered down to the street floor, and out the door they scampered. They both had their sights to visit the top of the Statue of Liberty, which they did, enjoying each other's company, and the fabulous sights as far as the eyes could see.

Without warning, Great-aunt Dora arrived at our home. Her intention was to invite Mother to accompany her to visit Germany for the summer. Mail even arrived around that time from other relatives, also stating, "Come! Come! Please come and join us. We are looking forward to seeing you!" She talked it over with her folks, and the subject was settled. Since it would only be for the summer, she would join Dora and visit the land where her parents were born. May it be noted that Caroline and Julius had to stay behind due to his very busy schedule. After all, he was a very dedicated physician not only to his work, but to his many patients as well. Mom spent some time readying herself for yet another trip across the Atlantic. In the course of a week, she left with her aunt where they found their way to the seaport and booked a voyage to Germany, upon the waters that carried with its chapters full of memories.

Mother relaxing on a park bench in New York City.

Chapter Four
Socialism Encounter

The sun had just set over the horizon with a circle of orange slowly losing its fullness, being swallowed up by the waters of the deep. In a matter of minutes, all that remained would be total darkness, not even a glimmer of light that brought division between the ocean and the sky.

Upon boarding, Dora and Mother were guided to a very nice room, with two beds and four windows overlooking the sea. Their voyage, a six-day transatlantic cruise, gave them plenty of time to visit the stately lounging areas or the dining halls adorned with luxurious furniture and palm trees; it was definitely a treat at best. This "country club setting" aided each traveler, as he or she were made to feel pampered on this trip across the waters.

During the daytime, many seafarers would walk the main deck to watch the seagulls fly above the vessel. Others loved to feel the breezes as coolness brushed against their skin as they grasped the rail, admiring the beauty of such peacefulness as gentle waves hit the side of the ship. The brownish waters touched off by sudden whitecaps were always a treat to see. The wave motions of the under forces of the tides would hold the eyes captive to a sea-traveling visitor.

As both ladies neared the German seaport, they thought they knew what to expect. After all, they had formerly made trips to and from the United States frequently. This time, it was shockingly different. No sooner did they near the seaport where the ocean liner was to dock, did they observe columns of marching soldiers. There were men in brown and black shirts, boys bearing swastika flags, girls in white blouses and tan skirts carrying banners. After they landed and disembarked, they could hear raucous speeches of the new National Socialists belching forth from radios as they walked past residences.

Uncle Joachim was quite bitter concerning the change of events. Some of Mom's school friends, however, were enthusiastic. When she saw them, for instance, they would greet her with "Heil Hitler." All the columns of marching soldiers made her long for the bucolic past when only the Catholics held processions at Whitsuntide, carrying the statue of the Virgin Mary and Jesus through the streets of Loerrach.

Another one of Mom's cousins, Hanna Steck, had recently married, she learned. Caroline and Julius asked her if she would be so kind as to join Mom and Dora as they took a trip across Germany. As a result, the three of them traveled to visit relatives in Nuernberg and Muenchen. It was there Mother had her first encounter with National Socialism. While deep in conversation with her cousin, on the Theatinerstrasse, a street in Bavaria, she felt a tug on her arm. As both of the women turned, a seedy little man could be seen mumbling something about a stiff arm. *A beggar*, Mom thought. Having a good heart, she was about to give him a few coins when her cousin pulled her away, bursting forth in perfect German with "We are foreigners!" After they had put some distance between the man and ourselves, Mom asked her, of course, "What was that all about?" Dora explained that they had passed by the memorial plaque affixed to the Feldherrnhalle, the field marshal's hall that commemorated the early Nazi fighters in the twenties, who had died there in confrontation with the police. As they turned to look back from where they passed, they saw everyone give a Hitler salute. This simple occurrence made them aware of the real changes that had taken place in the year since she and her parents had been out of the country.

More and more, Mom became sensitive to the different sounds of the streets—the recurring goose-stepping storm trooper boots pounding the cobblestone, the accompanying bands, and the ever-recurring singing of the Nazi "Horst Wessel" song. They could not feel but a bit eerie as the three of them walked together, sensing all that was going on around them. With the red swastika flags fluttering from most houses and the uniformity of the storm troopers' uniforms, not one of the threesome could escape the impression very similar to that of a stage performance, such as watching The Rockettes at Radio City Music Hall.

They ended their journey together in Oberammergau, a small village along the Ammer River, known for its wood crafting, where they witnessed the Passion Play. Even there, the many swastika flags dominated the little town, but not the performances, which, at that time, still told the story of Jesus. After they viewed the dramatic presentation, they exited the theater and continued walking on that same street. Eventually, they ascended a hill called an "Alm" in German. Coming upon a field, they decided to lie down among the tall fragrant grasses, listen to the nearby cowbells, and experience a great feeling of serenity and peace that Mother said she had ever known for a long time. Upon departure, Hanna was much relieved to return to her husband. Just as she was leaving, they were informed that an American daughter-in-law, Cynthiana Emcy, lived nearby. In no time at all did they find out where she resided, made contact, and spent some time together. "We all had such great times," Mom said, "took beautiful walks through the green meadows to harvest mushrooms, and drank wine cooled in a romantic little spring in the woods. The forests resounded with their happy toast to one another."

Many mornings, Mother would rise very early, much before any other of the people she was staying with, and roam through the woods alone. Her family said laughingly, "We were drunk with the love of nature!" That was the beauty of summer. She felt compelled to be among the unknown, from little flowers, to many shaped leaves, not to mention the tall timber that poked the puffy clouds as their branches jutted out to the heaven above. When Mom was there last, it was spring. Now, she found herself amid a new season. In no time at all, autumn had arrived, much to her surprise. As per agreement, she only intended to spend June, July, and August there.

Already being October, the last thing on her mind was returning to America. Being immersed in the beauty of her surroundings was a complete distraction to her. As she and Great-aunt Dora sat looking out a large window of a home belonging to Manfred—Uncle Alwin's oldest son, whom she met years ago—deer could be seen grazing along the pathways where the green grasses remained in the shadows of the pines. As they both sat comfortably, supping on cups of tea, a conversation occurred whereby Mother couldn't help rehashing her turning twenty-one, the official age whereby one becomes an adult. As a send-off celebration for her trip to their native country, her parents sprung a surprise birthday party for their "little girl," inviting some of her friends, the elevator operators, and Platt family members. Mom felt she definitely had achieved a new rung on the ladder. It was very much like some of the others, some in Germany, and others in America. She was treated with a three-layer cake, a beautiful new dress, and a hat that was so fitting for that era. There was a feeling of togetherness of the Fabricius family.

During her last visit to Germany, she was able to spend some time with her Uncle Alwin, a forester. Now that she was back in this country she was blessed, so she thought, with the opportunity to stay a number of days with one of his oldest sons, Manfred, who was also a forester. Since Mom had known most of the family well, she thought this gentleman would be as outgoing as the others. She was a bit surprised to find that he was a quiet man. Since he was not present upon her last visit, she became friendly with him, hoping he would come out of his shell and feel at ease talking to her.

One of the places Manfred took Dora and Mother was a little village hidden in a valley. At the last count, Gastbeiter was the home to approximately seventy-nine residents. When they walked over the top of a mountain and down a hillside, figures could be made out in the distance. Within seconds, a delightful odor of smoke was being sensed by the visitors, emanating from valley residents having fires to remove the chill in the air. The farmers sat around their hearths and were thankful for their harvests. As the four of them cozied up to the fire joining the others, Mom was starting to get some vibes that this forester who accompanied her was very fond of her to the extent that he wanted to marry her. She, on the other hand, was not in love with him. It was very hard to have feelings for anyone who seemed so quiet and depressed most the time. On the other hand, she did want to become a member of his family and the wife of a forester, so without much thought behind what she would be saying, she agreed to be his wife.

After becoming engaged, both of them took lovely trips throughout the fall, to the boisterous Duerkheimer fair, to the villages where the vineyard keepers sat in the inns sipping the previous year's wine while the last rays of sun were perfecting the grapes for the new harvest. The vineyards had just officially closed. This meant that anyone caught trespassing could actually be shot. The owners looked apprehensively up to the sky lest hail or heavy rain might ruin their crop. Tensions were everywhere. It was felt by everyone, including Mother. Thinking more and more as to what she impulsively committed to, she realized she made a commitment to a man she only knew too briefly, one who sat silently, letting merriment surge around him, drinking steins of beer. She actually disliked the beverage, not to mention the smells that accompanied it.

These odors mingled later on in her memory as part of the oppressive image of her soon-to-be-partner, which weighed heavily on her as they made plans to return to America. Although she affectionately addressed his father as "my beer uncle," she never thought of his drinking as being offensive. As for Mom, she took it in stride. They both got a chuckle out of his mischievous twinkle in his eye, and his hearty laugh accompanied by his frequent toasts. Summing up the facts of this whole situation, Mother quickly surmised that "The glass of beer was a prop in an actor's hand. In his son's, it seemed to be an essential part of his whole being."

Uncle Alwin's family situation was not great. Mom learned that they had lost all of their savings in the cruel 1921 inflation. Since that time period, they were determined not to "give new tears to old sorrows," and not to emphasize earthly goods. As head forester, Mother's uncle would never know want, and the huge garden and the venison of the woods provided them with culinary delicacies. The area's wine and the Bavarian beer flowed copiously. They lived like kings of old, happy in the beautiful unspoiled countryside and the forests that they husbanded. Was this also reminiscent of Mom's life on the farm? Perhaps. But her other lifestyle refused to be disposed of. She was no longer the seventeen-year-old escapee from boarding school, but a young woman who had sampled the cultural delight of a big city. Interestingly, while she was there, Mother was convinced she would like nothing better than to live in that little village where the tinny bell on Sunday enticed black, shrouded women and men to church. At such times, her uncle would say in good humor, "The Christians are ting-a-linging again, let us go into the forest to worship!" This was an invitation we enthusiastically could accept.

One day, on an outing through the meadows, however, an occasion took place that, for the first time, stunted Mom's affection for her uncle, and made his son appear in an even more unfavorable light. A puppy which had just been purchased as a future hunting dog was put on a leash. Immediately it balked and commenced to whine as it was pulled forcibly along. As her uncle yanked impatiently, the howling increased in intensity. The sound upset both Dora and Mom, and both of them tried to implore him to desist, but he finally ran even faster with the howling dog behind him. Later it was found that the poor creature had a good-sized abscess under the collar. No one displayed any remorse at this discovery, neither did the man she had promised to marry. That night Mom was unable to sleep, it upset her so. "Was I really cut out to be a forester's wife," she asked herself.

The time came for Mother to return to the America. The goodbyes this time were not tearful. She definitely was looking to head back home once again, and the reconnection of family and friends. No sooner did she board the train right after a festive sendoff did it develop engine trouble, and she feared not getting to the seaport in time to board the ocean liner. Fortunately, the problem was fixed in short order and she made it to the ship in the nick of time. As the vessel left and headed toward New York City, Mom would do much more than just eat and sleep on her journey. During the days, as she sat on deck chairs overlooking the ocean and the colors of the changing skies, she would have plenty of time to do a lot of thinking, sifting through the events and occurrences that took place over the summer not to mention the fall, as well. Hopefully, this excursion would help sort out all her true feelings.

The SS Europa *often transported Mother to Germany and back to New York.*

During the second day of sailing on the endless waters, as Mother awoke, it didn't take long to sense that the weather was anything but pleasant. A storm rose up, creating high waves that rocked the boat all day. She stayed in her cabin, accompanied by three Jewish girls who were emigrating to America. When the clouds broke, and a ray of sunshine peaked through, it became known that the bad weather was a thing of the past. Still burdening her thoughts was her uncle's son proposal and Mother's acceptance to marry him. That became overshadowed when she came under the spell of a young man from Holland. The ever-changing beauty of the ocean had always been exciting to her, but now she saw in these boundless waters a world apart, one that freed her from all continental ties.

When the boat arrived in New York, both Mom and her new friend, James Heide, were very much in love. She gave her fond friend a small tour of her famous city before heading over to see her parents. After introducing him to them, one could tell that they were pleased with her foreign friend and invited him to dinner. Since he spoke both German and English fluently, he made a very good impression on both of them. Soon, however, he would have to say his goodbye to both Mother and her parents, as he was on a tour of the United States. It turned out that he had been sent by his father, who owned a lumberyard, to educate himself on American timber. Nothing was ever mentioned about Mom's engagement to the forester.

The time had arrived for Mom to write to Manfred. Under the influence of her first intoxication of being really in love, she threw passionate words of regret on paper, expecting, no doubt, that the pure flame of love would defuse the family's condemnation. After sealing and stamping the envelope, she felt a load off her shoulders. What she didn't expect was what she got in return. Not even the letters of her traveling lover could mitigate the pain she felt over the contents. Manfred wasted no time in sending letters back to her. He refused to believe what she had written and was convinced she would retract her silly remarks. His father, on the other hand, called her a tramp, who had debased their hospitality in order to indulge in a light summer flirtation. Even though these were shocking words to her, they were evidence of a supportive father whose son had been hurt by her.

Julius compounded the situation by demanding she write to the parents and son and insist that Mother's chastity had not been violated on the ship. Mom was deeply hurt at her father's complete lack of faith in her. She realized she was very much alone, having lost the affection of her beloved "family" and being, as always, misunderstood at home. A good night's kiss after an evening of dancing did not need such defense. But her parents had to consider their relatives, and the attack by her uncle had been a strong one, and they felt it deserved and even stronger rejoinder.

Toward the end of December, Mom's traveling Netherlander returned to New York. Anxious to meet up with him again, she went down to the seaport during a bitterly cold evening to link up with him. Being that the city was all decorated for the season, the two of them took great joy rushing from Saks to Tiffany's, buying gifts for his sisters. While shopping, they each bought the same record for themselves titled "Can it be a dream, the joy supreme, that came to us in the gloom." That became "their song." Since he had already booked a room at the Waldorf Astoria, it was there during the evening they spent time dining and dancing once again.

During that time, Aunt Dora wound up in the hospital with a case of pneumonia. As a result, Mom was asked to watch her family. Right away, she realized she had little housekeeping skills. Not possessing siblings, she found this challenge a blessing in disguise. Inasmuch as there was plenty of work to do caring for three lively little girls, her thoughts would not be so much with the love she recently lost but giving them continued attention. If she decided to revisit Germany once again, this would certainly become a very healing activity.

While pondering her last visit during the summer to spend time with the forester's family, Mother had to mention to Alwin of her dream to be a good singer. She recalled of his speaking of a sister who taught voice lessons in Wiesbaden. Thinking it would be a positive act, she pleaded with her parents to allow her to return to Germany and study under her guidance with the main purpose of improving her skills. She had no ambition to become a professional singer. They consented.

Thus, Mom went forth "where angels feared to tread," once again following another small birthday celebration arranged by her parents in June. They saw to it that two dozen friends of the family attended the gathering. The next morning, she would be transported by her father's chauffeur to the seaport where he hugged her and sent her on her way. Buying a ticket, she boarded the ship, turning around once and waving at the family's driver. Her vanishing act took less than five minutes as many others did the same thing, lined up behind her, all looking forward to their upcoming journey.

Instead of leaving, with acts of memories weighing her down, she was now heading to Europe with great anticipation, hoping that God would bless her with insights of how to manage her future, wondering what this music instructor might look like, and would her goals be met, particular singing the scales from low to high "C." Her enthusiasm grew as SS Europa got closer and closer to the foreign seaport. On the sixth day adrift the battering waves gave way to a calmer water. Before one knew it, the ocean liner made way to the pier, the vessel docked, the gangplank lowered, and hundreds of people streamed down onto the dock and went on their way.

Mom took her time as she could see no need to hurry. No sooner did she get "grounded," was she met surprisingly by Cynthiana Emcy whom she wrote to tell her she was returning to Germany and would be arriving in the latter part of the month. Embracing each other joyfully, they left together sharing the merriment of each other's presence. The two could be seen climbing into a car that would take them to the home of her sister in the eastern part of the country where Mother would stay for a few days. From there, her journey took her to Wiesbaden where her new teachers greeted her. "Wie geht's," Frau Muehlhausen, referred to as Frau M., stated, upon seeing her new student. Standing right beside her was her husband, known as Herr M. In days to come, she would discover their powerful voices in their singing songs by German composer Wilhelm Richard Wagner. After Mom sang to them, she imagined that Frau M. must have thought, *Why did my brother send her to me for lessons?*

On the second day, she was introduced to the third member of the family, Heinz, his doe-like French bulldog. The two of them would parade around the large living room. His companion was trained with perfect precision, eager to please by healing, lying down and responding to orders on command. Then a piece of chocolate was offered, and Mother heard Frau M. distinctly say, "Haben haben [have have]." To her surprise, he did not receive immediately the chocolate. Instead, she heard the words, "From a Jew," and she watched Heinz turn his head away. When "From an Arian" was announced, he snapped up the reward. Mom realized right there and then, she found herself in the midst of Nazis.

Mother (left), pictured here with her long cylindrical container, is one of many residents of Germany who were waiting patiently for their one-pot dinners.

Chapter Five
Hitler's Artworks

There was nothing in her upbringing or experience that prepared Mother for anti-Semitism, or any anti-ethnic group, as far as that goes. As a small child, she remembered strolling along a beach on the New Jersey shore with her mother and coming upon an artist who had created a sculpture in the wet sand. Above it he had written, *The Huns.* "Who were the Huns?" Mom asked her mother.

"They were Barbarians who pillaged Europe hundreds of years ago. This artist meant the Germans." Caroline hurried her away. Her distress made it clear to her that she, as a German, was hurt by this reference. When the idea of discrimination arose, Mother was perplexed as she was uninformed as what the reasons were for anti-Semitism. As a matter of fact, the whole performance of Heinz ceased to be entertaining. She was actually to hear many more incredible utterances, thoughts that would convince her that National Socialism was a passing aberration. She thought Germans were intelligent people; but to her surprise, she was wrong. She recognized that some Germans could be much more concerned about and civilized toward their dog than toward humans of different races or ethnic backgrounds.

It was clear that the Muehlhausens were extremely fond of Heinz. Because of him, his master and mistress referred to each other as "Herrchen" and "Frauchen." This custom of Germans—childless couples who had dogs—of affectionately addressing each other of "little master" and "mistress" was not unknown to her. But here was a tall, well-endowed, Wagnerian couple who were neither small nor cute, as the diminutive form "chen" implied. Mom was never invited, nor did she care to address either one in this fashion. Eventually, however, she succumbed to call him "Herrchen" behind his back derisively! This had to do with his political theories, which she found utterly childish and boring.

It didn't take long for Mother to decide to call her "Frau M." and him "Herr M." For Frau M, she had an all-abiding, long-lasting affection. Her warm heart was to provide her with support, and her achievement filled Mom with admiration. She was not only a fine singer, but she also loved to paint and even tailor her husband's suits. On days when Mother would visit for instruction, and they would study *Leider*, Mom realized that Frau M. also had a sensitive poetic soul. The instructor's assignment of trying to teach the foreigner to sing required the skill of a sculptor, who creates a piece of art from a simple rock. In spite of Mom's feelings of inadequacy, she always looked forward eagerly to each new lesson. "We must first cure you of your hooting, tooting, and blowing," Frau M. exclaimed.

Herr M. would also teach her. He actually had a glorious, crystal-shattering voice. Mom's uncle had told her of his being engaged to sing in Bayreuth at the time of the First World War, a medium-sized city in the northern part of Bavaria. As a major in the German army, he sustained a lung wound that ended his career. Perhaps, this explained his bitterness, possibly even suggesting why he became an early fighter for National Socialism. He proudly displayed his golden party membership card. Sometimes, Mother thought, *What a tragedy for the world that Hitler could not have sold his mediocre art; then he would not have felt the need to set the world on fire—perhaps.*

Frau M's voice had a telltale tremolo. Her brother blamed her husband for insisting she sing one of Wagner's pieces. Before each lesson, it seemed Mom had to listen to *Traf Ich Das Schiff Am Meer,* from *The Flying Dutchman* or other Wagnerian arias. This was an exercise in futility, one to which Mom could not relate. Envy was totally absent from her reaction. She did not covet such a sound. Mom wanted to sing *Lieder* in a small pristine, clear voice, as some of composers of *Lieder* intended them to be sung.

The room in which Mother stayed was their former "Salon," a huge gathering place. It contained an enormous crystal chandelier in which she was allowed to burn one sad, lonely light bulb. Everything in the apartment bespoke of bygone wealth. Indeed, she heard frequently from their sons, August, the eldest, and Klaus, that before the inflation wiped out their fortune, there was money set aside for each child to take a trip around the world at the age of twenty-one.

House help was provided by the National Socialist regime. Muehlhausens had one female, Gretel, who accommodated their wishes. The "Hausfrau" was obligated to teach country bumpkins the rudiments of housekeeping in exchange for their services. This was one of Hitler's better ideas. Mom felt sorry for her, as she had to go down to the basement and fetch buckets of coal for all the rooms. It was not an easy job, and there were very little thanks.

Another one of Hitler's social innovations was the so-called "Winterhilfe" (winter aid). The money raised was supposed to assist the poor. Once a month, each family was asked to serve a one-pot dinner and give the money thus saved to the government for the poor. One could also avail oneself of a traveling soup kitchen provided by the army. Trucks carrying huge cauldrons of stew were located at street corners. Since Mother's lodging did not include meals, she often stood in line with her little pot to receive her Sunday dinner. There were times she did have money enough to pay for the meals. She did not realize, however, that instead of the money going to the poor, it went toward munitions. Did Muehlhausens know? This and many other questions remained unanswered.

Frau Ing attended many "Frauenschaft" (women's wing of the Nazi Party) meetings. It sounded to Mother as if it consisted of Red Cross courses, at which first aid, childcare, and women's health were taught. All she was assured of was that it was a part of making German women healthier, happier homemakers and mothers. They also learned to roll bandages.

She was not in Wiesbaden very long before she realized that music had taken a second place to politics with the Muehlhausens. Before each lesson, she received an indoctrination course in National Socialism, which for her, went in one ear and right out the other. She was truly not interested in the political structure of this new Germany. In the beginning, she did feel very grateful to them for taking so much trouble in trying to teach her how to sing and felt obligated to listen to their political views. But gradually, however, their perceptions began to bother her, for she felt her father was not paying money for her to have a course in political science.

Mother contemplated going back home. On second thought, she did recognize that her reason for coming was to better her singing abilities. As a result, she decided to stay on and learn more that would benefit her singing abilities. She spent the month learning to breathe from her diaphragm and to forgo any singing of her favorite *Leider.* She could actually note that a new voice was being created. Herr M. lured her to unexplored heights on the scale, where her teachers discovered she had a potential in this "virgin territory above the note C." She heard herself screeching the notes, but she didn't care. To her they were delightful. "That was the first step to producing a healthy note," they explained. She also was told that she had to be of a "blasen" aptly translated, this meant producing a breathy tone—one that caused Barrett to howl just like the dogs do when the fire whistle sounds. One day they said they would leave it with Mom. And as predicted, it did quite a bit of howling that afternoon.

Learning how to sing became an engrossing experience. When a former very-talented pupil, with a beautiful soprano voice, came to visit Frau and Herr M., Mother was told that this person had no idea how she produced the rich tones that soared so majestically. Instead of envying her, Mom pitied her, for she would never know the thrill that she was experiencing. She definitely came under the spell of these masters of Bel Canto who had promised her a voice. She knew she would never be engaged, as the visiting soprano was, to sing at the Charlottenburger Opera in Berlin, but she told herself she had the intense pleasure of being "in" at the beginning of creation of a voice. Her former mode of singing had to be obliterated. "Listen to a baby cry!" said Herr M. as she produced this sound. She was actually aware of an understanding of what singing was about. She expected to react viscerally rather than intellectually, both in politics as well as in voice production. Her instructor repeatedly reprimanded her by stating the words, "Stop thinking so much!"

There was a willingness on a part of Mother to listen to a baby's crying in order to understand her true voice, but she refused to think as a little child in order to comprehend Herr M.'s "Weltanchauug." "National Socialism," said Herr M., "was the government of the future. Democracy was outdated. It had proven to be ineffective. The masses were always wrong, and the government by the people, of the people, and for the people was plainly an anachronism."

When Mom spoke mightily of enlightened voters, he only scoffed. "Look," he said. "What 'Der Fuehrer' had accomplished in this short period, it would take a democracy three times as long with so much waste and inefficiency. We have the greatest, most efficient government on earth." At what cost to human lives, Mom had no idea at that time.

The sound of the stormtroopers boots as these struck the cobblestones and the endless singing of the "Horst Wessel" song made her aware that she was no longer living in the Germany of her childhood. She could not stand the raucous speeches of "Der Fuehrer" on all the radios. At times, she felt she was in a foreign country where they happened to be speaking German. She had no desire to contact old friends from Loerrach. It would be difficult to explain that she would be back in Germany for the purpose of studying singing. She certainly had not been given evidence of possessing an unusual voice when she attended school there. She also remembered her visit to that town the previous summer, when their enthusiastic espousal of National Socialism made her feel once again like an outsider. They had certainly gone divergent ways in the intervening four years. How would she have foreseen that this alienation would disappear many years later after the war, when she again would find the same, gentle, kind friends she had known in her childhood. Her stay in Wiesbaden lacked all continuity to the past. As she looked in the mirror, she asked the young girl with the puzzled expression, "What in the world are you doing here, taking lessons from two Wagnerian singers who want to turn you into a coloratura soprano and a Nazi?"

The answer to this question came at the end of that week when Mother received a letter from her love in Holland. He suggested they meet in Koeln (Cologne), a city in Germany. Once again, fall had arrived. In fact, the anniversary of their meeting was imminent. For a brief moment, the invitation rekindled memories of great happiness on the ocean liner. But unlike last summer, which she had characterized as lighthearted, she thought of the past months as another boot camp, like the first weeks of boarding school. Instead of a happy rendezvous or an invitation to visit Holland, she found herself enrolled in a basic course in voice production and political indoctrination. "Forget how you used to sing, think, or act!" she heard, coming from either Frau or Herr M. "Free yourself of all former concepts—vocally, philosophically, and politically!" The unfilled, romantic expectations were conducive in creating a dedication to Mother's studies, as frustrating and infuriating as they sometimes seemed. It was not an easy decision to agree to this meeting. After all, the invitation was long overdue. But as emotion takes the heart of the soul, she went.

What began to linger in Mom's mind as she boarded the train for that city was the memory as having had hours of expected joy, thinking back of their shipboard experiences. Once on land, she met him with open arms, grasping his hand. The two of them would then visit many area attractions. They watched the barges drift by on the Rhine, many of which she would remember for the rest of her life as bearing the initials "NL," standing for "Netherlands." As they stood there gazing hither and yon, each entertained the other with numerous stories, Mom with her humorous past experiences. They were definitely happy together. No doubt was left in her mind of any diminution of his love.

As Mother stepped off the train in Koeln, each welcomed the other with outstretched arms and clutched each other as though they hadn't seen each other for years. He quickly grasped her possessions and the two headed to a restaurant where the "lovebirds" would catch up as to times gone by. Two hours later, Mother would check in into the five-star Excelsior Hotel Ernst. They would meet Saturday morning at a place of their choosing.

Morning came quickly as the rising sun highlighted the buildings just outside one of the windows of her large bedroom. Knowing that the day would be full of surprises, she hurriedly bathed, dressed, and collected possessions for yet another rendezvous. Grabbing the room doorknob, she quickly turned around to see if anything was forgotten. Then rotating the brass device, she opened the door, and exited her luxurious quarters and made haste for the place they thought would be a nice quiet place to start off the morning's activities.

And as always, when the both met up, the usual took place, the outreach of arms, hugs by them both, small pecks on the cheeks of the other. They then clasped each other's hands, turned one direction or the other, and walked and talked. Both days included visitations to many gift shops, a stopover to watch an operatic stage performance, not to mention wining and dining at some of the most eloquent restaurants in the area. In Mom's mental scrapbook, many more pictures were squeezed into the remaining pages.

As she could only stay for a short time, her departure grew nearer. The days went by quickly. The time had come, and she was escorted by her "lover" to the train station. As she watched the train arrive, it stopped, the doors opened, and immediately the conductor lowered the step stool. As she climbed upon the first step and then to the next two, she anticipated, very possibly, an invitation back to Holland. Instead, what she heard, in a matter of minutes, as the train was about to leave the station, left her in shock. His words rang out, "I cannot see you again!" he bellowed out. The outrage at his waiting until the last moment to tell her this extensively diminished her joy and left her stunned. Even on the whole trip back, she was bewildered upon words. To say that Mom looked shocked arriving at the station in Wiesbaden was an understatement. One thought surfaced, and that was the emotion of her uncle's son receiving the letter stating that the engagement was off as she did not want to see him anymore. Mom felt this was her punishment, for as Goethe said, "All wrongdoing is punished right here on earth."

Having arrived back to the location of her singing lessons, she had mixed feelings of returning. Yes, she was there to improve her vocal abilities, but not to learn how to become a Nazi. Leaving the one who she thought loved her a lot, only to be told not to see him ever again, was not in the cards. The only way to put joy back in her heart was to now concentrate fully on what her intentions were when coming to Germany, and that was to improve her singing.

Frau and Herr M. were no doubt keenly aware of Mother's inability to produce notes of their standards. That week turned out to be a nightmare, for he, sensing her vulnerability, embarked on a veritable crusade for National Socialism. He chose this moment to enlighten her on the true nature of Moses, which he claimed his latest research had revealed. "That clever fellow used gunpowder on Mount Sinai," he said, "to fool the people into believing God had spoken."

Whereas up to now, Mom had allowed his political "words of wisdom" to go into one ear and out the other, she reacted irritably to this ridiculous statement. Vaguely, Mother remembers asking him, just what was this supposed to prove? "Is it that the Ten Commandments are to be invalidated or that Moses is indeed to be considered a very clever fellow?" she asked. This was the beginning of a pitched battle between Herr M. and herself. One fact was clear. The void created by her recent loss would most certainly not be filled with a passion for National Socialism! A greater resolve to learn how to sing did rise to the surface. Herr M.'s political lectures suddenly became a godsend, however. They lent a bit of comic relief to her personal tragedy. There were more stories like one about Moses. All lacked credibility. Sometimes, she even wondered whether he had not also suffered some brain damage during the war. It was because of his farfetched theories that she did not take the Nazis seriously. Germans were far too intelligent, she thought, to accept such fanciful ideas.

Mother did not tell the Muehlhausens what happened to her on her weekend trip to Holland. In the past, Herr M. used to share stories about his former pupils' affairs before each concert. Knowing this made her realize she would tell him nothing as what had happened. Sooner or later, singing lessons would include advice on love, from his point of view, of course, of National Socialism. Mother overheard Herr M. saying that Hitler welcomes babies, just so they were Arian. Young people were encouraged to overthrow the parents' morals and follow the dictates of their hearts. I don't think her singing teacher proposed to mother to have a baby, but definitely to have an affair.

Still in thought was why her friend from Holland left her. She tossed around the idea in her mind whether or not she should write to her "lost love" and demanded an explanation. All kinds of thoughts ran through her mind. "Why did my former love who contributed so enthusiastically toward creating a festive day when he had come to visit terminate their relationship? Mother thought about taking the next boat to New York, but it was almost as though the Muehlhausens had cast a spell on her with their bel canto singing. She concluded that they sensed her dedication to music. But it was surmised, that they both felt that their goal was to cure her of her introspection.

It didn't take much to convince her that their non-analytical minds allowed them to be swayed by a man like Der Fuehrer. "You are stuck in the past!" screamed Herr Mother, objecting to his simplistic theory that Christianity was not a suitable religion for Germans. It was designed to weaken the German youth. Too much emphasis is on "love thy neighbor." "Love an Aryan," she said sarcastically. She was never a proselyting Christian, but it did seem to her that "love thy neighbor" was the basis for all civilized relationships between individuals and nations. It was later that Mother realized that almost every major religion expressed this thought in one way or another.

She had not so much as a hint that war would be in the very near future. Certainly, the Muehlhausens never let on that it was coming. However, the sons of her landlady, students of law and medicine, hinted at such a possibility. Their whole family was not at all enchanted by Hitler. The law student actually told delicious political jokes, any one of which, he assured Mother, could have gotten him into a concentration camp if uttered to the wrong person. She enjoyed their companionship very much; it was like having a brother she never knew. Most evenings, however, she spent time alone, reading books. November was rainy and dreary, and since she opted not to practice singing, instead, she read and memorized the lyrics to songs. Admonished by her landlady for using too much electricity, Mom decided to crawl under a huge comforter, in her lovely antique Biedermeier bed, and try to fall asleep so as to numb the thoughts of her lost love who daily lingered in her mind.

Mother (left), with a group of school friends in Germany.

CHAPTER SIX
DROWN THEM

It was December, shortly before Christmas, when the mailman brought Mom an envelope with an unmistakable stamp from Holland. Inside she found a most surprising letter, which stated that her former love regretted having tried to kill the most precious thing in the world: love. "Could we meet during the Christmas holidays?" was the next sentence. She was never to know what her life might had been had she given a favorable response. Was it pride, the kind that commeth before the fall, that caused her to write that she was spending a holiday with her aunt?

Of course, she should have insisted he come to Wiesbaden, but her thoughts of the last months far outweighed her memories of the past. "Her heart had become a fossilized shell," as the cynical Joachim Ringelnatz said in a poem. She spent a miserable week with her doting aunt, who attributed her pallor to poor nutrition, and who set about restoring her good health with her hearty cooking. Ensuing correspondence with the Hollander lacked spontaneity. There was something forced and false from then on in their writing to each other. He did not come, and she did not encourage it. She began to see their love as it was described in a song, with a partial stanza that came immediately to mind, *just a dream, the joy supreme that came to us in the gloom,* one to be cherished forever, in spite of the unhappy ending.

As National Socialism grew in Germany, Mother knew that the Nazis were keeping an eye on her. She became known as a student of singing from the United States. Her mail was not only under watch, but each time she left town, she had to let the police know as well when she returned, requiring signing in upon her arrival. She had not antagonized Herr M. to the extent that he would have threatened to inform the authorities, so she moved about with a confident knowledge she was actually "a student from America," even though Frau M. spoke of her as a "returning German."

Periodically, Mother was invited to partake in Sunday dinner in the formal dining room where the old porcelain stove appeared in decoration only because of the cost of heating it. The room was cold. As a result, all who attended were attired in winter coats. Taking a bath was also a teeth-chattering experience. She was permitted a few inches of hot water, produced by an instantaneous heater on the wall. Of course, the room contained no stove, and there was no need for a curtain since frost on the windowpanes provided perfect privacy. She soon realized she was the only user of the tub, and she subsequently availed herself frequently of the mineral baths in the cellars of the hotels. There, however, she did not soak in the heavenly hot water either after an experience of being joined by a huge water bug that plunged heroically to its death next to her.

In the same hotel, an English club met once a week, and she decided to join. The members consisted mainly of a few Germans and the sons of the Oriental carpet merchant who were from Pakistan. There were also a few English visitors. The president was a British soldier from the First World War who had married a German girl and stayed behind. This balding little man fancied himself a playwright, and she was soon to be his leading lady. A one-act play had to do with an American manufacturer of pork and beans who wooed an English noble lady. There was much ado about the ratio of a little bit of pork to a lot of beans. The final classic line was "Thelma, give me your lips!" Fortunately, the curtain was lowered before she gave her consent.

One time, she went to his house to get a script and met his sad wife and their three fragile-looking children. Mom became aware of the apparent poverty under which they lived. His sole income, it appeared, was derived from teaching Jews who wished to emigrate to America. It was obvious that this was not adequate. Only after the war ended did Mother learn from Frau M. that he was a spy for

England, and as the tides turned against him, he was shot and killed. Saddened and baffled by this news, she wondered, *Is the show of poverty just a front?*

One of the members of the club was an English singer. She sang popular songs in hotels and was really a very pleasant person. Mother soon found out that the entertainer was very much in love with one of the sons of the carpet merchant who had taken a liking to her. At this point, she felt inclined to leave the club. She did not want to interfere with the romance.

February bought Fastnacht—Mardi Gras. All Wiesbaden went wild. It seemed to her that no one went to work during that period, and the wine flowed day and night. There were balls in the hotels and in the Kurhaus (health resorts). Mother, accompanied by the English club, attended one such ball. She had no intention of masquerading, but a hairdresser suggested he pile her hair into a peak, spray it, and sprinkle little stars on it. Inasmuch as it suited her budget, she agreed to let him do it.

Actually, she found the event to be rather boring. In retrospect, it was far too soon after the end of her romance. She was not ready yet for such hilarity. At one point, the young teller from the bank, from whom she always procured her checks from home, rushed up to her with a lovely young girl in his arm stated, "You a woman of the world! Tell this pretty young thing to go to bed with me, woman of the world!"

Oh, how I wished Herr M. could have been there to hear this! Naturally, she warned the pretty young woman that she was in trouble, but it was Fastnacht. Everyone giggled, and nothing was taken seriously. It was the pleasant young English singer who sent Mother home long before the party was over. Hours after she had gone to bed, she heard two sons of the landlord enter the building; they too were part of the merriment somewhere else. Singing lessons resumed shortly thereafter. Mom was thrilled when she heard that her favorite song that she loved to sing so much would be included on the list of pieces to practice. On one mild spring day, when the windows were open, Frau M. said, "Close the window. I have a Mendelssohn song I think you would like, even though he is a Jew."

By then, another soprano pupil had arrived, and both she and Mom sang duets. This not-too-young singer had acquired some bad singing habits. She boarded with some nuns and was, therefore, in Frau M.'s eyes, not to be trusted. She thought this girl was a spy for the Pope. Why did this idea not seem bizarre at the time? Was it possible that she was slowly absorbing the National Socialism paranoia? The girl did seem rather strange to Mother and very unwilling to share any confidences. A matter of fact, she did not stay very long and was not missed when she left. Mom felt that being the only student at this time was not unhealthy.

In May, Frau M. suggested that Mother take a test at the local conservatory. It was called an "Eignungspruefung," which roughly meant, a "qualifying exam," one that would permit her, were she a German citizen, to continue studying with the idea of becoming a concert singer. These tests were, no doubt, all part of a well-organized new Germany where no young person would be permitted to waste his/her time in some idle pursuit. She and Mom prepared carefully for the examination, and to her great joy passed and received a very formal piece of paper, which stated that she could go on studying to be a *Lieder* singer. Considering her humble beginnings of being a young "Kate who sings out of the kitchen window," she was greatly encouraged.

Herr M. still made fun of her prudishness and showed it in ways she did not appreciate. One time, he jumped from the piano and planted a kiss on her cheek with such gusto that a red mark ensured. Frau M. questioned whether she had been eating strawberries. Mother was not impressed with Herr M.'s demeanor. Underneath his Falstaffian exterior, she suspected there was a pampered little boy; his pockets had to be checked by Frau M. whenever he left the house to be sure they contained money for the tobacco he set forth to purchase. His behavior right after the war bore this out.

In hindsight, Mom doubts that she ever was foolish enough to indulge the fantasy that her in-the-laboratory-constructed voice would find acclaim. But she was satisfied when she was able to sing a musical phrase to Muehlhausen's satisfaction.

The summer brought some social contacts—some old, some new. Mom's old friend, Max Cornelius, from the Platt School of Music, came from New York, and they took a trip down the Rhine to Koblenz (Germany). He was resolved to sing *The Lorelei,* a lyric by Heinrich Heine. When they approached the famous mountain where the notorious sire, according to legend, fishermen were lured to their death by this enchanting song. This "folk song," much beloved by generations of Germans, now noted: lyrics by anonymous. Heine was a Jew. Evidently, Mother and Max were too eager to defy the Nazis and sang the song the first time to the wrong mountain; it had thus to be repeated. The visit was a heartwarming event marred only by Herr Walt's boorish behavior. When Max sang for Frau, he heard from the neighboring room Herr screaming, "That is no baritone. That is a tenor!" Sometimes Mom felt that antisocial behavior was further evidence of weakness. She made the mistake, thus again, of drawing the conclusion that National Socialism was supported by misfits and would, therefore, not endure for long. In retrospect, she was very glad the two, Max and Herr M., never met, as Mother was sure Herr M. would not have missed the opportunity of enlightening him on the great Fuehrer and Moses. She would have not liked her friend to think that she was an understudy for a big role on the National Socialism stage.

Some weeks later, Mother invited her landlady for a trip on the same boat. She thought that would cheer her up. This, however, turned out to be a total failure. At the time, she knew nothing about her philandering husband. Now, she realized that her depressed condition had something to do with the fact that she may have suspected her absence from home just made his flirtation that much easier. It was while Frau M. and Mom were walking Heinz on one of the more secluded paths that they spied the loving couple. She was a baroness known to Frau. Mom said she was sure they were never seen by them. From that day on, however, she formed a strong disliking for the little lieutenant colonel, for she was very fond of his sad, overworked wife. Subsequent events later in the year made her suspect he actually had seen them and knew she was a witness to his indiscretion. She could not think of anyone else who would give false information to the authorities about her, thus hastening her departure from Germany. At the time, Frau M. and Mom had a slight chuckle about the whole thing, and then it was forgotten. Not long thereafter, Mother had an encounter of sorts with the old guard military establishment, an episode so absurd, it could have been written by her friend, the English playwright. The widow of her landlord's former commanding general and her son were frequent guests. She was a delightful aristocrat whom Mom had the pleasure of inviting to sit under her impressive chandelier while she awaited the arrival of the rest of the family. The three great flights of stairs were no small feat for her to ascend, and Mom was truly concerned since she was a fragile, elderly lady. When the sons came home, they were all excited and asked if Mom had addressed her as "Excellency?" She said, "No." She called her, "Gnaedige Frau (madam)," having been brought up to consider this the proper way of addressing a genteel, elderly lady.

Frau M. was not the problem; it was her son, Klaus, a man in his early thirties, who was known to be slightly deranged. It was rumored that his marriage had lasted exactly three days. Since he was a music lover, Mother did accept his invitation to attend a concert. It was obviously not pleasant always to go alone. He arrived, smartly attired, sporting a silver-capped cane, offering her his arm in the most gallant fashion. Wanting to comply with his bit of cheer, she projected her left hand in and around his arm so as to couple the two arms together. Both turning around, he led her out into the hallway, she pulling the door closed behind her. From there, they walked merrily down the steps and out into the street. It was approximately five blocks to the concert hall. Once there, he paid for the tickets and with smiles on their faces they entered the large auditorium.

She enjoyed the music very much and told him so. Happy to hear those words, he subsequently invited her to more concerts as well. When he expressed his feelings, one could tell they came from the heart. Thinking there was a strong emotional tie evolving between the two of them, he suddenly proposed to her on one of those outings. Taken aback, she knew she had to be very careful in her response. She knew she had to reply with as much gentleness as possible. That same evening, she made the mistake of telling this to her landlord's sons, one of whom found it necessary to tease Klaus. What ensued was a ridiculous melodrama, for he insisted she appoint someone to fight a duel with pistols in order to restore his honor. It was all a rather sad farce, and Mother sought the Muehlhausens' help. Their suggestion for her to write a polite letter to his mother was a good one, for she answered it in a kind and understanding manner. Thus, the matter ended. Mom was noticeably upset, however, with the landlord's son who had created all the disturbance. She felt he could have risen to her defense. He, however, stated that this was impossible since it involved the son of his father's former commanding general. It was all an anachronistic foolishness that left her less impressed with her landlord's sons and their rather absurd pretense of being tied to the past.

Other friends of their family included a young girl, Lilo, who was Mother's age, who was engaged to a strapping SS man, who was a member of a paramilitary organization under Adolf Hitler. Her mother, also an army widow, was a "golden button" National Socialist like the Muehlhausens. Mom had very little in common with Lilo, but she promised to teach Mother how to knit—a deficiency she felt from time to time. During these lessons, she told her all about her preparations for marrying her illustrious fiancé. Being blond seemed paramount, and her mother being a "golden button" party member certainly did not hurt (her Arian ancestry, of course, had long ago been established). She had nude photographs taken of her from all angles. The pictures would be entered into an archive of super men and women and their expected-to-be-perfect progeny. To Mom's surprise, the wedding date was set in the not-too-distant future. The ceremony and reception would take place in a Protestant church, no less.

When the big day arrived, family and friends could be seen filing in, one by one, through the large oak-colored doors. It was a quaint house of God that contained no more than forty pews featuring a small altar with an eight-foot bare cross hanging above it. Sitting on the middle on the cloth, strewn across the table, was a large gold chalice in the middle with two thin candles, which were lit. Their flames did their little dances as the breezes could be felt ever so little, but just enough to add comfort to the premises.

As a hymn was sung, the bride was escorted to the front of the church. Trumpets blasted away as she got midway down the aisle. There was slight turning of heads as eyes gazed and followed her to the front where she would soon unite with her husband-to-be. It was all very beautiful, the church itself, the transmission of their feelings for one another, and exchanging of rings. Mother was mystified that there was never a sound of an organ playing. She was told afterward an organ was not an appropriate instrument for the occasion since its origin had been from the orient. Thinking back, she remembered very little about the ceremony. In fact, she couldn't recollect if a pastor was even present.

Mom was not invited to the reception, which did not bother her. After returning home and eventually going to sleep, she was awakened by calls to her from the street below. This was one of those instances that always brought a smile to her face every time she thought about it. It so happened that after the sons returned from the celebration and gotten home, they forgot to take their keys and were so hoping she would hear them. "Could you please throw down our keys?" one hollered as Mother opened the window to see what all the noise was about. In her semi-wakeful condition, she omitted to wrap them in some cloth. Even though their size was formidable, they were not easily found. Watching the inebriated sons combing the poorly illuminated cobblestones was compensation for having been roused from slumber. Their gratitude the next day was understandably mixed.

Later, after the war, Lilo obtained Mother's address from the Muehlhausens. She wrote a pitiful letter, pleading for assistance. It appeared that her illustrious SS man had abandoned her and their two children and had run off with her young cousin. Since Mom had many family members to consider first, she sent the newlyweds whatever what was left over in food and clothing. "So much for the master race!" she said.

During the summer of 1936, Mother was suddenly asked to buy black material to cover her window. She knew only too well that this was not in preparation for Halloween. The Olympic Games in Berlin proclaimed peace on earth, goodwill to men. What message did the blackout drill give? She was completely taken aback by this happening. One night in Leuteburg became dark; SA men (the assault division of the paramilitary organization under Hitler) checked to see if any rays of light were visible. The Muehlhausens assured her that this was necessary inasmuch as this and many more drills would be carried out as a way of preventing enemy aircraft from being able to identify their targets by sight.

The blackout drill did not really frighten her as it should have. Mother carefully avoided writing to her parents about it, for she had no desire to go back home. Singing lessons were just beginning to go well—relatively speaking, of course! Her life contained no new headaches, and she resented the thought of a war interfering with her harmonious existence in Wiesbaden. Her repertoire was beginning to grow; she remembers singing "Mimi's Aria" from *La Boheme* and thinking how funny it was. One phrase required great dexterity of the tongue. She would imagine Cid Caesar, with his facility in speaking rapidly, doing justice to the words crowded into the music. In Germany all operas were then sung in German. Some translations were better than others.

It was in the fall, and Frau M. suggested Mother take another "Eignungspruefung," this one for the opera. It would be given in Frankfurt. The preparations for the test were far more elaborate. She had to submit a short biography and a photograph, which had to be taken in a studio. After viewing her picture, she had to admit, it had a touch of glamour. Mom felt a bit uneasy, for she felt that it showed what appeared to be a confident young girl of whom much more might be expected than she knew she had to offer. She voiced her concerns about taking this test to her teacher. Mother was told, it did not matter if she did poorly; it would be a good experience.

She prepared a Mozart *Aria* and some Schubert. Also rehearsed were some political answers, for Frau M. stated one never could tell what might be asked. Mom memorized the slogan: "Gemeingut geht vor Eigengut," roughly translated, "The wellbeing of the community must take precedence over that of an individual." Then there was, of course, the quotation that National Socialism, i.e., "Der Fuehrer," had overcome communism and reactionism. One more item was about women: "A German woman does not smoke or use makeup." There were many more.

She took off to go to Frankfurt with some trepidation. When she entered a large hall, she was confronted by two men and one woman sitting at a table. As she approached them, one man said right away to her, "It appears you are not aware of what has taken place in the last years in Germany!"

"Oh, yes," Mom said. She was politically knowledgeable; she had been given some answers by her teachers.

"Well," said the other man. "You must know that Jews are not welcome in the Third Reich." He thought she was Jewish.

"Oh," Mother stated, "I am not a Jew.

"Ha," said the lady. "Anyone coming from America can say that!"

Standing her ground, she fired back, "But I have an Arian passport. All my relatives are in Germany, and they too have Arian passports."

An Arian passport was a document in which one entered the names of one's parents and grandparents. For each name, one had to supply a Christian baptismal certificate. One took the documents to the proper authorities and received a stamp over each name. The Muehlhausens had suggested she procure such a document. Since Mom's uncle had given her the appropriate document, it was no problem at all. It seemed of little interest to the three examiners. They had formed an opinion and had no intention of changing it. At the time, it did not occur to her, but later she did realize someone had deliberately misinformed them, for how else would they have come to such a conclusion? *Was it that someone wanted her to leave Germany?* she pondered. It became obvious that her being an American was in itself distasteful to the three examiners.

"Well," said the lady at the table, "now that you are here, you might as well sing."

Mother's concentration, so important in preventing her from slipping back into her former way of singing, was utterly decimated.

As she embarked on Zerline's *Aria* from Don Giovanni, she heard the trio's loud conversation, and she smelled the smoke from their large cigars. She was not permitted to complete the singing, for one man shouted, "Stop, stop, this is enough! Come here!"

She did as told. Then the other asked her, "How much are you paying for the lessons?"

She told them.

"Take that money to America, and take cooking lessons with it!"

This was the end. The examination had lasted a very short period, and she was back on the streets of Frankfurt in a dazed condition. Her very first thought was that she had let the Muehlhausens down. She had sung poorly. Surely the examiners did not continue in believing she was Jewish after my mentioning the Arian passport. Without doubt, her singing was inadequate. Characteristically, she questioned her abilities as she had done from early childhood.

As Mother reached the bridge over the river, Main, she looked down at the moving waters and allowed some of those self-deprecating thoughts to float away. In their place an idea arose. Could it be that she, indeed, was Jewish? Maybe she had been adopted. Was this the reason she was unable to feel utterly "Duetsch" anymore? Was there something in her physical makeup (now referred to as genes) that predetermined her way of responding to National Socialism? Had her picture that preceded her appearance before the Board given some hidden evidence to the examiners of her being Jewish? Herr Walt had already called her a "Judenfreund" (friend of the Jews). He also had made the statement, which, of course, she considered a typical Herrchen foolishness, about earlobes being different in Jews. Instinctively her hand went up to her ears, but then dropped quickly. How absurd it all was. It would have been much easier had she been a convinced anti-Semite; she simply could have felt outraged for having been mistaken for a Jew. As it was, she was simply confused by what had just happened to her. She had never before been treated this way through no fault of her own. It was a new experience, one she found very unpleasant. What if she were to find out she really had Jewish blood? She could not imagine that it would matter to her. What had these dreadful men momentarily done to the cohesiveness of her personality at that moment? Why was she wandering aimlessly through the streets of this city, asking herself all these foolish questions? She felt befuddled and very alone. Mom was a refugee in a foreign country, certainly not a returned German American. She believed at that time her empathy for persecuted humans was formed. For a brief instance, she had been one of them. She had walked in their shoes.

Suddenly, Mother found herself in front of a movie theater where, of all things, Shirley Temple was the star. Impulsively, she decided to go inside. She had no idea what she expected this charming little girl would do for her, but as it turned out, what she accomplished was a bit of a miracle. The youngster she portrayed, sang, and danced her troubles away and somehow took Mom's with her. Inherent in the movie was a free American spirit—a belief in new beginnings, something she needed very much at that stage. She was able to identify with this young actress—as an American.

After being "reborn in the spirit," so to speak, she exited the theater and headed toward the railroad station. Her more determined gate gave evidence of a resolve. In a little less than forty-five minutes she was on train that would transport her back to Wiesbaden. Over the mechanical noises of the engine could be heard the sounds of the tracks as the wheels rolled over them. The conductor punched the tickets as he neared her seat. Her glimpses of the goings-on outside the rectangular-shaped windows weren't as serene as she remembered when she entered this country in the early thirties. And even though there was much distraction, many thoughts went through her mind about just what the future might bring.

When the train entered the station, it stopped. Mother carefully stepped down onto its platform. Noticing that the sun was just setting, there was just enough light to get her bearings. Gathering her belongings, she made her way home. Making way to her room, she was happy to have returned. Plopping down on her bed, her eyes toward the ceiling, she pondered over what had just transpired, gradually dozing off to sleep.

The next day Mom met with her singing teachers. In no time at all did she express fury at what had occurred. She suspected, possibly, the Muehlhausens of filing the complaint that led to her treatment.

On the other hand, she withdrew her thoughts when she surmised that they couldn't have done such a horrible thing. There was, however, a conflict raging within her. If it wasn't them, then who were those who would have the audacity of assuming control of her life? At that time, she didn't want to believe that someone had deliberately misinformed the examining board about her being a Jew. Would it have mattered? No, for she already made plans to leave Germany.

How will all this be resolved? Mother thought. "It was simple. All along, plans were being made to be home for Christmas. Now would be the perfect occasion to leave. This time she took no lengthy farewell trips to relatives and friends. Before she departed, she did visit her cousin, Hanna, in Muenchen, who had just given birth to a son. He would become Mom's godchild. After having a friendly visit, rehashing some of the fond memories that they experienced together, Mother greeted them farewell and headed for the train station in an effort to travel to Hamburg. Just as it was, many times in the past, her sights were seen as making way to the seaport to board the ocean liner and set to sea.

Buying her ticket, possibly for the last time, and walking up the plank to enter the deck of the ship, she was conflicted. Did she bear a melancholic mood or one of happiness just to free herself from the challenges that tore at her being on a day to day basis? All was erased, as now, any ambivalence she might have had about leaving had vanished. She would start thinking about how she would be received particularly by her parents. Would they prepare a festive meal for their prodigal daughter? She had come as a stranger and was departing as one, leaving a country she could no longer call "my Germany." This time she was truly emigrating as three Jewish girls in her cabin had done.

As she walked, peering in the various places to gather, it became evident, there were few passengers on the ship. Since socialization was not on her mind, she had more time to view the brooding skies and the dark and ugly sea. Most of the time she spent traveling home was in her cabin. Loneliness was not the problem. Having a seedy, middle-aged traveling salesman dogging her every step became the culprit. When the vessel reached the seaport in New York, her thoughts turned to her family and the future.

The day before the boat landed, Mother began to anticipate her reunion with her family and friends. All those who were her age had graduated by then from college. Mom had only her "Eignungspruefung" certificate in hand and an unfinished voice. Fortunately, most everyone had likely forgotten her original reason for her trip to Wiesbaden. The recent events in Frankfurt and her ensuing disillusionment with Germany cast powerful signals, drowning out the Holland incident, even for her. Returning to New York was less traumatic this time than when she was seventeen. There were no longer any ties to Germany and no surprises to greet her.

Soon, it became apparent that she and her father would not revert to their former adversarial relationship. Her docile behavior, however, could be attributed to an abysmal apathy. There was some thought in her mind of seeking a new vocal teacher. Her voice seemed to have collapsed. As her sole attachment to Germany lay with its poetry, she decided to go back to school and become a German teacher. Through old musical friends, she had the good fortune to find a singing teacher who understood she had only a peripheral interest in improving her voice and wanted to enjoy her favorite *Lieder* instead. Mother would eventually become a highly recognized teacher of German.

After she had returned, Mom had given a great deal of thought to the importance of her life of that period of time in Wiesbaden. Along with the purity of tone, the Muehlhausens tried to chisel her defused voice and help her fine-tune her thoughts. There actually was a relationship between the two! The robust, healthy, sometimes-punishing atmosphere had cured her "Peur de Vivre" (fear of life). The intolerance of her signs of weakness and their insistence, she knew her own mind, all were disciples carried forward from the days of Hilda Ohrwurn. Daily, she ran the gauntlet of Herr M.'s derision and was comforted, in turn, by Frau M.'s affectionate nature. She was finally able to strike back when the subject of National Socialism surfaced. Thus, even the negative aspects of her experiences were important building blocks of her character. When she finally left Germany, she no longer wondered whether she was a potential Netherlander, a returned German, or an American. There had been pain and disappointments during those three years, but these had been necessary so that she could cease her wanderings and put down roots in her native land. Mother supposed that she even owed a debt of gratitude to the examiners of Frankfurt who forced her to make the decision to leave.

She wondered if Herr M., himself, had not set the whole process in motion because of her increased belligerence toward National Socialism. Perhaps too he had realized she never would bring him fame with her insignificant voice. Better to forgo the Havana cigars her tuition money provided than have it be known he harbored a "liberalistisch verseuchte Schuelerin" (a polluted liberal student). One day, he had actually thrown a book at her while screaming this epithet. At the time, this meant little to her, for it would take years to even understand what a liberal was, let alone a polluted one.

Frankfurt was an eye-opener. There she realized that anti-Semitism was not just a hobby of Herr M. It appeared to permeate the whole political system and placed power over individuals in the hands of people with small minds. She truly did not know then how these very small minds and ultimately sadists would bring about the so-called solution. Previous to her experience, she asked Herr M. how he visualized solving the so-called Jewish problem. He said, "Drown them in the Red Sea!"

"Typical ravings of this silly old man," she foolishly concluded. Mother naively believed that concentration camps were used for people who opposed the Nazi government, only some of whom were Jews. Of mass deportations of Jews to concentration camps, even of individuals being molested, she was uninformed, for her social life in Wiesbaden was too limited. All she knew was that Jews were leaving Germany since they too took English lessons from the "Playwright"?

Even though Mom knew she had to leave Germany, she did admit that it was not an easy decision to make. She realized how dependent she still was on the Muehlhausens, vocally. They were, after all, the creators of her voice! Would anyone else take the same interest? She doubted it. The time had come for her to cease indulging in her fantasies.

Frau M. composed a farewell poem for her. The opening stanza compared a human being to a globe. If one turned the globe around, one could gain a different perspective—a more pleasing one, perhaps. Mother understood her analogy too well. She seemed to find certain traits of hers annoying, but she had taken the trouble of discovering more favorable ones. There were, however, loving good wishes tucked away in the stanzas. She seemed to feel that if she truly persisted, someday, she the pupil that she was, would have a small but resonant voice that could rise to the rafters of a concert hall. Now that, alas, she was leaving, she saw her hopes disappear.

Much had to do with her obstinate refusal in accepting National Socialism. The Muehlhausens had at first hoped she might consider becoming a member of the National Socialist "Fifth Column," called "The Bund," when she returned to the United States. It was obvious that the "complex" side of her character could not be counted on to fulfill this mission. This had to do, she intimated, with her propensity for "gruebeln" (brooding), which was not a true German characteristic—in any case—not an Arian one. Too many doubts prevented decision-making and led one to overlook the important issues.

When World War II broke out, Mom was in college and engaged to a German, Ernst W. Volkmann, who had come to America in 1926. Through him, she acquired a whole new family in Germany, along with her relatives and some of her old friends, who depended on her for food and clothing when the carnage of the war had ended.

After they married, Mother and Dad moved to Pittsburgh, where both would establish themselves in their trades. In a matter of time, three of us would be brought into the world, I would be the oldest to set foot on this earth, and then Bob and later Elizabeth, or Betsy, as she is commonly referred to, were born. Over the many years, we too became nomads, eventually establishing roots all over the world. Julius and Caroline would settle down in Bethel, Pennsylvania. My parents and I also lived in the commonwealth, a few miles from each other; they were in the Ligonier area of the same state, until their passing, and I in Latrobe where with my wife, Teri, raised a son, Aaron and daughter, Kelsey. Bob and his wife, Rita, would settle in Mystic, Connecticut, where they would they brought up Jeffrey,

Jonathan and Elizabeth, and Betsy and her husband, Leigh, would find themselves living in his home country of New Zealand, where they too would reestablish their roots and bring into the world Ryan and Andrew.

Throughout our upbringing, Mother would often sing lullabies to the three of us, from our very early ages, until we were a bit older. Her music lessons did pay off, in a manner of speaking.

She still remembers one day in Pittsburgh when someone asked her, "Where are you from?"

She quickly responded, "I'm a New Yorker!"

The very simplicity of her answer surprised her. It seemed somewhat dishonest, she felt, since she actually had been such a nomad. But as she had pointed out in her writings, "How easy it had been in Loerrach so many years ago when 'I come from America' had been my answer to the question, 'And where are you from, little girl?'"

Beatrice Caroline Fabricius, 20, 1934

IN REMEMBRANCE...

"Out of the mystery of life we have come and into it we return. To look out into the stars in the deep of night is to feel the vastness of space beyond our view, to feel infinitely humbled; yet how much greater than the stars, and more wonderful than space and night, is the miracle of human life! Here in this tiny corner of the universe we know a mystery more profound, a glory more sublime than all we know or guess about the stars. For here within the mystery of flesh is worked the miracle of mind and love. This is the greatest wonder of them all, beside which, our little knowledge is a paltry thing, dry dust beneath the living flesh of a truth so great we dare not even guess at it.

"And greater than earth and stronger than flesh is the spirit of man, and greater, we dare to hope, than death. For spirit is the off-spring of eternity—child, comrade and coworker with eternal forces which have created us. In its wonder, somehow, we feel that it transcends all words of birth and death. Let not thy heart be troubled seeing that this thing comes to all men and all flesh, for things that are of flesh must perish after the way of the flesh. But the spirit is more wonderful than these. Pain cannot subdue it nor disaster destroy, and we who mourn do but bear witness to the glory which shall rise again."

—Beatrice Caroline Volkmann

CPSIA information can be obtained
at www.ICGtesting.com
Printed in the USA
BVHW090525021220
594419BV00008BA/128